CONVERSATIONS
WITH SCRIPTURE:
THE GOSPEL
OF MATTHEW

Other Books in the Series

CONVERSATIONS
WITH SCRIPTURE:

THE GOSPEL
OF MATTHEW

JOHN Y. H. YIEH

Morehouse Publishing
NEW YORK · HARRISBURG · DENVER

To my parents:
Ing-Chu and Liu-Chih† Yeh
Yung-Huei Cheng† and Shu-Yuan Su
Rev. Gene and Betty Koelker
who love God's church with their whole heart

Morehouse Publishing, 4775 Linglestown Road, Harrisburg, PA 17112

Morehouse Publishing, 445 Fifth Avenue, New York, NY 10016

Morehouse Publishing is an imprint of Church Publishing Incorporated.

www.churchpublishing.org

Series cover design by Corey Kent

Series design by Beth Oberholtzer

Typeset by Kerry Handel

Library of Congress Cataloging-in-Publication Data

Yieh, John Yueh-Han.
    Conversations with scripture : the gospel of Matthew / John Yieh.
        p.   cm.
    Includes bibliographical references.
    ISBN 978-0-8192-2420-0 (pbk. : alk. paper)
    ISBN 978-0-8192-2835-2 (ebook)
    1. Bible. N.T. Matthew—Criticism, interpretation, etc.   I. Title.
BS2575.52.Y54   2012
226.2'06—dc23
                                                    2012004560

Printed in the United States of America

10 9 8 7 6 5 4 3 2 1

CONTENTS

We thank you, heavenly Father, for the witness of your apostle and evangelist Matthew to the Gospel of your Son our Savior; and we pray that, after his example, we may with ready wills and hearts obey the calling of our Lord to follow him; through Jesus Christ our Lord, who lives and reigns with you and the Holy Spirit, one God, now and forever.

AMEN.

INTRODUCTION TO THE SERIES

To talk about a distinctively Anglican approach to Scripture is a daunting task. Within any one part of the larger church that we call the Anglican Communion there is, on historical grounds alone, an enormous variety. But as the global character of the church becomes apparent in ever-newer ways, the task of accounting for that variety, while naming the characteristics of a distinctive approach becomes increasingly difficult.

In addition, the examination of Scripture is not confined to formal studies of the kind addressed in this series of parish studies written by formally trained biblical scholars. Systematic theologian David Ford, who participated in the Lambeth Conference of 1998, rightly noted that although "most of us have studied the Bible over many years" and "are aware of various academic approaches to it," we have "also lived in it" and "inhabited it, through worship, preaching, teaching and meditation." As such, Ford observes, "The Bible in the Church is like a city we have lived in for a long time." We may not be able to account for the history of every building or the architecture on every street, but we know our way around and it is a source of life to each of us.[1]

That said, we have not done as much as we should in acquainting the inhabitants of that famed city with the architecture that lies within. So, as risky as it may seem, it is important to set out an introduction to the highlights of that city—which this series proposes to explore at length. Perhaps the best way in which to broach that task is to provide a handful of descriptors.

The first of those descriptors that leaps to mind is familiar, basic, and forever debated: *authoritative*. Years ago I was asked by a colleague who belonged to the Evangelical Free Church why someone with as much obvious interest in the Bible would be an Episcopal priest. I responded, "Because we read the whole of Scripture and not just the parts of it that suit us." Scripture has been and continues to play a singular role in the life of the Anglican Communion, but it has rarely been used in the sharply prescriptive fashion that has characterized some traditions.

Some have characterized this approach as an attempt to navigate a *via media* between overbearing control and an absence of accountability. But I think it is far more helpful to describe the tensions not as a matter of steering a course between two different and competing priorities, but as the complex dance necessary to live under a very different, but typically Anglican notion of authority itself. Authority shares the same root as the word "to author" and as such, refers first and foremost, not to the *power* to *control* with all that both of those words suggest, but to the capacity to *author creativity*, with all that both of those words suggest.[2] As such, the function of Scripture is to carve out a creative space in which the work of the Holy Spirit can yield the very kind of fruit associated with its work in the Church. The difficulty, of course, is that for that space to be creative, it is also necessary for it to have boundaries, much like the boundaries we establish for other kinds of genuinely creative freedom—the practice of scales for concert pianists, the discipline of work at the barré that frees the ballerina, or the guidance that parents provide for their children. Defined in this way, it is possible to see the boundaries around that creative space as barriers to be eliminated, or as walls that provide protection, but they are neither.

And so the struggle continues with the authority of Scripture. From time to time in the Anglican Communion, it has been and will be treated as a wall that protects us from the complexity of navigating without error the world in which we live. At other times, it will be treated as the ancient remains of a city to be cleared away in favor of a brave new world. But both approaches are rooted, not in the limitations of Scripture, but in our failure to welcome the creative space we have been given.

For that reason, at their best, Anglican approaches to Scripture are also *illuminative*. William Sloane Coffin once observed that the problem with Americans and the Bible is that we read it like a drunk uses a lamppost. We lean on it, we don't use it for illumination.[3] Leaning on Scripture—or having the lamppost taken out completely—are simply two very closely related ways of failing to acknowledge the creative space provided by Scripture. But once the creative space is recognized for what it is, then the importance of reading Scripture illuminatively becomes apparent. Application of the insight Scripture provides into who we are and what we might become is not something that can be prescribed or mapped out in detail. It is only a conversation with Scripture, marked by humility that can begin to spell out the particulars. Reading Scripture is, then, in the Anglican tradition a delicate and demanding task, that involves both the careful listening for the voice of God and courageous conversation with the world around us.

It is, for that reason, an approach that is also marked by *critical engagement* with the text itself. It is no accident that from 1860 to 1900 the three best-known names in the world of biblical scholarship were Anglican priests, the first two of whom were Bishops: B. F. Westcott, J. B. Lightfoot, and F. J. A. Hort. Together the three made contributions to both the church and the critical study of the biblical text that became a defining characteristic of Anglican life.

Of the three, Westcott's contribution, perhaps, best captures the balance. Not only did his work contribute to a critical text of the Greek New Testament that would eventually serve as the basis for the English Revised Version, but as Bishop of Durham he also convened a conference of Christians to discuss the arms race in Europe, founded the Christian Social Union, and mediated the Durham coal strike of 1892.

The English roots of the tradition are not the only, or even the defining characteristic of Anglican approaches to Scripture. The church, no less than the rest of the world, has been forever changed by the process of globalization, which has yielded a rich *diversity* that complements the traditions once identified with the church.

Scripture in Uganda, for example, has been read with an emphasis on private, allegorical, and revivalist applications. The result has been a tradition in large parts of East Africa which stresses the reading of Scripture on one's own; the direct application made to the contemporary situation without reference to the setting of the original text; and the combination of personal testimony with the power of public exhortation.

At the same time, however, globalization has brought that tradition into conversation with people from other parts of the Anglican Communion as the church in Uganda has sought to bring the biblical text to bear on its efforts to address the issues of justice, poverty, war, disease, food shortage, and education. In such a dynamic environment, the only thing that one can say with certainty is that neither the Anglican Communion, nor the churches of East Africa, will ever be the same again.

Authoritative, illuminative, critical, and varied—these are not the labels that one uses to carve out an approach to Scripture that can be predicted with any kind of certainty. Indeed, if the word *dynamic*—just used—is added to the list, perhaps all that one can predict is still more change! And, for that reason, there will be observers who (not without reason) will argue that the single common denominator in this series is that each of the authors also happens to be an Anglican. (There might even be a few who will dispute that!)

But such is the nature of life in any city, including one shaped by the Bible. We influence the shape of its life, but we are also shaped and nurtured by it. And if that city is of God's making, then to force our own design on the streets and buildings around us is to disregard the design that the chief architect has in mind.

—Frederick W. Schmidt
Series Editor

NOTES

1. David F. Ford, "The Bible, the World and the Church I," in *The Official Report of the Lambeth Conference 1998,* ed. J. Mark Dyer et al. (Harrisburg, PA: Morehouse,1999), 332.
2. For my broader understanding of authority, I am indebted to Eugene Kennedy and Sara C. Charles, *Authority: The Most Misunderstood Idea in America* (New York: Free Press, 1997).
3. William Sloane Coffin, *Credo* (Louisville, KY: Westminster John Knox Press, 2003), 156.

AUTOBIOGRAPHICAL NOTE

I grew up in a Presbyterian church in Taiwan, where Christians are a tiny group surrounded by Buddhists, Taoists, folk religionists, and atheists. Getting along with others in a multireligious society requires me to define my Christian identity with clarity, to live a Christian life with integrity, and to negotiate with the dominant culture with sensitivity. Not unlike Matthew, in order to prove the church's validity, Christians in Taiwan have to live an ethical life with higher distinction to command respect from our neighbors. There is social pressure for us to be the salt and the light.

In college and graduate school, I participated in interdenominational fellowships and began to appreciate the wide range of experiences and traditions that each church has to offer to the common witness to God's kingdom. Loving each other in creative tension can be a blessing from God. Indeed, as an ordained Minister of the Word and Sacraments in the Presbyterian Church (USA), I feel privileged to serve the Virginia Theological Seminary as a professor of New Testament to train future priests and leaders for The Episcopal Church. For sixteen years, I have been joyfully immersed in Anglican tradition and daily Episcopal services. Ecumenical experiences have enriched my understanding of the Bible, theology, and worship, and enhanced my research and teaching. Inviting my students to think cross-culturally and ecumenically often affords them new perspectives and fresh ideas and leads them to a sharper sense of Episcopal identity and a deeper appreciation for the Anglican contributions to the whole church as God's people.

I began to take interest in Matthew's gospel twenty-five years ago, wanting to learn about the person and thoughts of Jesus. Many of Jesus' sayings are preserved in Matthew, and his teaching has a transformative power to change believers' lives and define the vision of the church. Then I began to study the Sermon on the Mount, examining its remarkable history of interpretation and influence. How can Jesus' high moral principles be appropriated in a postmodern society? This is a serious issue on which the church needs to deliberate. Jesus commands his disciples to live an alternative way of life as a witness to the kingdom of heaven. Following Jesus is costly, but God's grace makes it possible.

In the last two decades, I have taught a seminar on Matthew almost every other year. My love of Matthew continues to deepen, because it is truly "the gospel of the church." Matthew's amazing story of Jesus has shaped the beliefs and practices of the church through centuries. It continues to call us to discipleship and offers guidance for the church to fulfill its mission. I hope our reflection on the major characters in Matthew's gospel may bring us to a personal encounter with Jesus at intellectual and spiritual levels, and lead us to recommit ourselves to following Jesus as his disciples in our daily life.

CHAPTER ONE

A New Gospel

Attending a memorial service is an intense spiritual experience. As we all know, bidding farewell to the deceased is emotionally draining, and no words of comfort are ever sufficient to sooth the grieving family. Oftentimes we simply cannot accept the fact that our loved one has gone. It is also true that, as we try to cope with the sorrow, the gathered family and concerned friends are vital supports. Their presence enables us to bear the unbearable, because they remind us that we do not have to face death alone. Prayers, scriptures, and hymns also bring some release, because they reassure us of God's promise of peaceful rest and eternal life. There is hope beyond death.

Eulogy performs a special function in the memorial service. It often provides a *curriculum vitae* of the deceased's family background, life experiences, and great accomplishments, and reveals memorable characteristics and special qualities of the person in the eyes of the family and friends. As we listen quietly to eulogies, vivid memories of the deceased will surge and episodes of past encounter will replay in our minds. Suddenly the person seems to have come back to life in our midst, and we are ushered into an experience of communion, a moment of grace that is authentic and heartwarming. Eulogies are informative, relational, and emotionally affecting, so they often bring laughter, tears, tranquility, and some catharsis to people in mourning.

To their readers, the gospels in the New Testament functioned like eulogies of Jesus. Of course, the authors of the gospels were convinced that Jesus had been raised from the dead, and they had experienced his powerful presence in their lives as Lord and Savior. Each author remembered, celebrated, and highlighted some aspects of Jesus' life and death for their readers; each had a special relationship with Jesus and held a particular perspective on his legacy. When we read the gospel of Matthew as a eulogy of Jesus, therefore, we get to know about its author as well as Jesus, and our beliefs and lives will inevitably be challenged and reshaped by its author's point of view.

Why Another Gospel?

Since the early nineteenth century, New Testament scholars have preoccupied themselves with the historical questions of who Jesus was and what he actually said or did in his life. To some, such as Bultmann, Crossan, and Borg, these gospels are "faith-tainted" reports, devoid of objectivity, so researchers have to play cool-minded detectives peeling off layers of post-Easter theological interpretations in order to uncover the core facts. Reading the gospels thus becomes a scientific process of evidence gathering, the kind of forensic analysis we see on television that reconstructs the scene of a crime. To them history and faith belong to separate realms; believers will need to take a giant leap of faith from history to confess Jesus as personal Lord.

Gospels contain historical reports of Jesus based on Christian experiences, so historical facts and faith interpretations cannot be clearly separated.

Other scholars, such as Bornkamm, Johnson, and Meier, acknowledge the mixed nature of the gospels, but they also insist that there is no such thing as objective history without personal prejudice or, at the very least, bias. Every journalist reports news from one point of view, every photographer shoots a picture from one angle, and every historian comments on an event with one perspective. Gospels contain historical reports of Jesus based on Christian experiences, so historical facts and faith interpretations cannot be clearly separated. Nor should they be, because Christian faith is not fantasy but commitment to Jesus Christ, the incarnate God who once walked on earth as a man. The one who proclaimed the kingdom of God from Nazareth and the proclaimed Lord of the church are the same person. These scholars thus propose to see Jesus through the lens of early church authors whose witnesses are recognized as partial but honest. In other words, they read the gospels as documents of history and faith, critically but not skeptically.

Regardless of their positions on the debate, most scholars agree to the following sketch:

- Jesus was a Jew growing up in Nazareth near Sepphoris, Herod Antipas' first capital city, and became a wandering teacher in Galilee, a fertile region in the southern part of the Roman Syrian province in the early first century.
- Like John the Baptist, who preached judgment and repentance by the Jordan River, Jesus announced the arrival of the kingdom of God and traveled from town to town to urge his compatriots, who interacted daily with Gentiles but took pride in their status as the chosen people of God, to change their lifestyle and do righteousness according to the law.
- He befriended sinners and tax collectors, debated with the Pharisees and the priests, and confronted hypocrites and money lovers.
- He performed miracles with compassion and power, healing the sick and casting out demons, so he attracted a significant number of followers.
- He initially chose twelve men to follow him as disciples, explaining to them the mystery of the kingdom of God and sending them on missions to proclaim his kingdom messages.
- While in Jerusalem, he was arrested and convicted as a blasphemer by the high priest and a rebel king by the Roman governor, and then was crucified.
- But his followers believed that he was raised from the dead, so they continued to talk about him and wrote down many extraordinary things he had said and done (see Luke 1:1–2).

After Jesus' departure, his followers began to eulogize him and share their memories of him with others. Some remembered his compassion and power in performing miracles, having been cured of painful diseases or freed from demon possessions. Others testified how their lives were changed by his incisive teaching on God's mercy and justice, or spoke of how their minds were enlightened by his fascinating parables regarding the mystery of the kingdom of God. Very soon, the stories of how the righteous Jesus suffered and died in the hands of Caiaphas the high priest and Pilate the Roman governor was recollected and written down in some detail to commemorate his innocent death and to explain God's purposes. It was thus that miracle stories, teaching discourses, and passion narratives came into existence. The early churches also used these sacred memories to defend Jesus' credentials as the Messiah, to preach his gospel of salvation, and to encourage believers to bear witness to him. In other words, it is in the efforts to justify their faith in Jesus under polemic, missionary, and educational circumstances that the early churches began to conserve and expand their eulogies of Jesus. Before Matthew composed his gospel, moreover, several oral traditions and written sources had already been established and circulated among the churches. Would it not be easier simply to make copies of those earlier eulogies? Why did he decide to write a new gospel? What did he hope to accomplish with it?

In one sense the author of Matthew did make "copies," using at least three earlier eulogies in order to compose his gospel. What were these earlier accounts he drew on? In 1924 the scholar B. H. Streeter at Oxford proposed the "four sources hypothesis," a theory that many scholars still support today, to explain the agreements and disagreements among the first three New Testament gospels (also known as the "synoptic gospels.") He meticulously argued that Matthew used the gospel of Mark as its narrative basis but expands it with sayings taken from two anonymous sources, Q and M. Q stands for "*Quelle*" in German and is a hypothetical source consisting of Jesus' sayings found in both Matthew and Luke. M refers to other materials available only to Matthew, while Luke also uses Mark, Q, and a further special sourced called L. Mark, Q, M, and L are thus the four earlier sources used by the two longer gospel accounts, Matthew and Luke.

Why do scholars believe that Matthew had access to Mark's gospel and used it as the narrative basis for his own? There are several important reasons.

- Eighty percent of Mark's materials occur in Matthew's gospel in exactly the same sequence.
- Mark's Greek has limited diction and simpler syntax than Matthew's, with stronger Aramaic influence.
- Mark gives a less complimentary portrayal of the disciples than Matthew does.

Given their massive similarities in contents and wording, therefore, Matthew and Mark most probably have a relationship of literary interdependence. But which is the source and which is a later rendition? Considering Matthew's more sophisticated Greek in terms of grammar and style, it is more likely that Matthew gave Mark some extra literary polish rather than the other way around. The more positive image of the disciples in Matthew also indicates his later date, on the ground that a later author would change his source traditions to honor rather than to embarrass disciples who, like Peter, have become respected apostles of the church. Matthew may also have quoted a great number of sayings of Jesus from the Q source, which includes over two hundred verses of sayings that reflect such distinctive themes as wisdom Christology, apocalyptic prophecy, and imminent judgment. It is true that no one can be certain whether these sayings were preserved in oral or written forms and how they became available to Matthew and Luke, but given the similarities, it is highly possible that both Matthew and Luke had access to this body of material. In short, Matthew probably knew Mark's gospel and the Q sayings along with his special source, M. So he decided to combine all these sources to compose a new and longer gospel. If we study Matthew side by side with Mark and Luke, this opportunity to compare and contrast brings his distinctive perspective and concerns into sharper relief.

Alone among the gospel writers, Luke states clearly that he has investigated his source materials and organized them into "an orderly account" so that his readers "may know the truth concerning the things" about which they have been instructed (Luke 1:3–4). His intended readers are novices who have been taught something basic about Jesus Christ; his purpose is to provide new believers with historical, reliable, and coherent knowledge of what has happened to Jesus so that their faith can be reinforced. For Luke, therefore, faith should seek to understand, while knowing historical truth is equally important to pursuing spiritual experience. John also tells his readers that he has chosen some most important materials in his disposal to report in his gospel so that they may come to *believe* that Jesus is the Messiah, the Son of God, and "through believing you may have life in his name" (John 20:31). It seems that John assumes that some of his readers are not yet firm believers, some might not yet be fully convinced that Jesus is the Messiah or the Son of God, and others might not know that believing in Jesus can bring them eternal life. That is why he hopes to show them who Jesus really is and what benefit the faith in him can bring. Like Luke, John considers reason and faith compatible and complementary to each other. Understanding helps bring forth faith, and believing in Jesus is key to eternal life.

Unfortunately, Matthew (like Mark) does not declare his intentions in the same explicit way. In order to find out why Matthew wrote his gospel, we need to look for clues in the way he presents the story of Jesus, especially as it compares with Mark.

How Is Jesus' Story Presented?

There are two methods of reading Scripture that can help identify the special ways in which Matthew presents his story of Jesus. The first is to look into the literary structure of the entire gospel to see how Matthew begins and ends his story of Jesus, and where he places the climax of the story. We should also look for repeated themes in the narrative that might reflect his special concerns or messages. In other words, we should look into the literary composition and narrative development of Matthew's gospel to see what the narrator tries to say (or hint) to his readers. Scholars call this "narrative criticism." The second method is to compare key "pericopes" (self-contained episodes or passages) that have parallels in Mark or Luke to observe how Matthew used the same materials in ways that may reflect his particular tendencies and perspectives. These tendencies and perspectives are then explored in the particular social-historical settings of his church to discover what his main reasons and purposes might be. This method of research is called "redaction criticism."

First of all, let us look at Mark's version, from which Matthew drew much of his story, for comparison. It is a relatively short story about Jesus' adult life with a focus on his death; one scholar has described it as "a passion narrative with a long prologue." It begins with Jesus' baptism by John and a powerful ministry in Galilee but appears to end anticlimatically with his crucifixion in Jerusalem and the discovery of the empty tomb. To some readers, it reads like a tragedy. It can be divided into two halves by geographical settings, Galilee and Jerusalem. Unlike Matthew's gospel, which begins with Jesus' birth, Mark begins with Jesus' adult ministry. Beginning with a citation from Scripture, he identifies John the Baptist as the voice in the wilderness who will herald the coming of the Lord, and suggests that Jesus' ministry in Galilee has indeed fulfilled God's promise to lead God's people on a new Exodus from exile back to God (Mark 1:2–3). Mark 1–9 tells the story of Jesus in Galilee, where he preaches the coming of the kingdom of God, exercises a stunning power to heal the sick and cast out demons, and claims a divine authority to forgive sins. With striking wisdom he also outwits the learned Pharisees and scribes over issues of the law. People are so amazed by his wisdom and power that they begin to wonder whether he might be the prophet of the end time, or the Messiah himself. A turning point takes place near the end of Jesus' ministry in Galilee, when he raises a serious question to his disciples in Caesarea Philippi: "But who do you say I am?" (Mark 8:29). Peter confesses him to be the Messiah, but immediately Jesus commands them to keep quiet about it and predicts three times that he must suffer and die in Jerusalem (8:31; 9:31; 10:33–34). Why must the mighty miracle worker in Galilee be humiliated and executed in Jerusalem? The answer can be found later in the narrative.

Jesus' predictions indicate that he knows very well that he will meet with rejection, suffering, and even death in Jerusalem, but he goes there anyway.

Jesus' predictions indicate that he knows very well that he will meet with rejection, suffering, and even death in Jerusalem, but he goes there anyway. His journey to Jerusalem is thus a conscious decision. Why is he willing to face death? Because he is convinced that his death has a higher purpose:

"For the Son of Man came not to be served but to serve, and to give his life a ransom for many" (Mark 10:45). His death on the cross will serve as a ransom to redeem God's people from their sins. The idea of giving up his life as a ransom foreshadows the mystifying words Jesus says to the disciples at the last supper about the bread and the cup: "Take, this is my body . . ." and "This is my blood of the covenant which is poured out for many." These words and actions evoke the Jewish custom of sharing the paschal lamb before the Passover commemorating God's miraculous rescue of their forebears from Egypt. The idea of serving even unto death also evokes the "suffering servant" of the Lord in Isaiah who will receive the Spirit of God to "bring forth justice to the nations" (Isa. 42:1–4). Like the servant, Jesus keeps silent before his accusers, is blindfolded and tortured, and is struck, spat on, and mocked. These close parallels to the Servant Songs of Isaiah in Mark's passion narrative indicate that Mark regards Jesus as the suffering servant who "poured out himself to death, and was numbered with the transgressors; yet he bore the sin of many and made intercession for the transgressors" (Isa. 53:12). In other words, Jesus may look like a victim of religious conspiracy and political expediency, but his death is voluntary and vicarious—the righteous Messiah who lovingly and courageously dies on the cross to save the sinful, and whose death will bring about the new creation. Like the paschal lamb that was sacrificed, he heralds the new Exodus for God's people. Like the suffering servant who endures rejection and tortures, he brings forgiveness and healing.

Mark's emphasis on Jesus' vicarious death matches the theological content of Peter's proclamation to Cornelius, the Italian centurion and God-fearer in Caesarea. Thus it is a fuller account of the early Christian kerygma, or message: "All the prophets testify about him that everyone who believes in him receives forgiveness of sins through his name"(Acts 10:43). In contrast to the popular expectation of the Messiah to conquer the world by the power of his mighty angels, Jesus changes the world by exercising his messianic mission with humiliation, suffering, and self-sacrifice on the cross. Why did Mark characterize Jesus as the crucified Messiah? One reason may have been the need to defend the church's faith in Jesus as the Messiah despite his apparent weakness and death in the hands of the Jewish leaders and the Roman governor. Jesus' voluntary death as a ransom to redeem the world offers a robust answer to the question of mockery from the priests and the scribes: "He saved others; he cannot save himself" (15:31). Mark may also have a pastoral reason. He wanted to reassure Christians under persecution in the Roman Empire that they have a sympathetic partner in Jesus, who has suffered like them but has conquered sin and death with perfect faithfulness to God and tireless compassion for people.

Let us now turn to Matthew's portrayal of Jesus to discover his purposes in writing his gospel. It contains the same stories of Jesus' ministry in Galilee and Jerusalem as those in Mark, but he adds other traditions such as the nativity stories, the five long discourses of Jesus' teaching, and an appearance by Jesus after the resurrection. Hence Matthew is both richer and longer. Rather than beginning as Mark does with the adult Jesus preaching and healing, he starts with Jesus' miraculous birth in Bethlehem. Jesus' "biography" according to Matthew can be divided into three major sections:

- Section 1: Family background, unusual birth, and special preparation (1–4).
- Section 2: Major thoughts, activities, and accomplishments in public career (5–25).
- Section 3: Suffering, death, and legacy (26–28).

In the earliest section Matthew draws on many new materials to introduce Jesus' special identity and role before he starts his ministry. By presenting a genealogy that traces Jesus' family line back to Abraham and David, Matthew tries to prove that Jesus is a legitimate son of David and thus the Messiah whom the Jews have long expected. With the story of Joseph's attempt to release the pregnant Mary from betrothal, Matthew highlights Jesus' unusual birth from the Holy Spirit that points to his identity as the Son of God. Adding the story of the wise men from the East seeking to worship the newborn king, Matthew foreshadows Jesus' relationship with the Gentiles and all nations. Most significantly, there are

> *In the earliest section Matthew draws on many new materials to introduce Jesus' special identity and role before he starts his ministry.*

several episodes—the slaughter of Jewish babies in Bethlehem, the holy family's escape into Egypt until God calls his son out of Egypt, Jesus' coming up out of the water after baptism as the heavens open, and his temptation by the devil in the wilderness for forty days—that parallel the well-known stories of Moses in the biblical narrative of Exodus. These parallels strongly suggest that Jesus is the new Moses who is the savior and lawgiver of his new people. The parallels reach a climax when Jesus walks up to a mountain to deliver the Sermon on the Mount, as Moses once led the people of Israel to make a covenant with God on Mount Sinai and receive the law to guide their life.

Most prominent in the next section are the five discourses that Matthew has compiled from Q and other sources according to their themes. These saying collections provided the author with Jesus' main ideas on ethical and religious topics, so they function as a summary of his teachings according to Matthew.

- The Sermon on the Mount (5–7)
- The mission to the Jews (10)
- The mystery of the kingdom of heaven (13)
- The preservation of church order (18)
- The preparation for the final judgment (24–25)

These five discourses take up more than a third of the entire gospel. Matthew considers them highlights of Jesus' ministry, so at the end of each discourse, we have the formulaic phrase, "Now when Jesus had finished saying these things" he went on to do something else (see 7:28, 11:1)—as if teachings were more important than healing the sick, debating with the Pharisees, or calling for repentance. It was not until he had finished teaching "all these things" (26:1) when Jesus was ready to be handed over to his opponents to be crucified. We should also notice the repeated warnings about the final judgment in each discourse, which says people will be judged by their response to Jesus' teaching: "Every tree that does not bear good fruit is cut down and thrown into the fire. Thus you will know them by their fruits" (7:19–20) and "Everyone therefore who acknowledges me before others, I also will acknowledge before my Father in heaven; but whoever denies me before others, I also will deny before my Father in heaven" (10:32–33). Thus Jesus is portrayed above all as the "one teacher" of God's will, with absolute authority and crucial significance for the final judgment.

The final section, beginning with Matthew 26, is a detailed report of Jesus' last week in life. He suffers betrayal by his disciples, arrest by the temple police, trials by Jewish council and Roman court, torture by soldiers, crucifixion with criminals, and death in pain. Most of these elements of the narrative are found in Mark, but Matthew adds remarkable stories of Jesus' resurrection from the grave, the Pharisee's attempt to lie about it, the reunion with his disciples and the Great Commission. On a mountaintop the risen Jesus declares to his disciples that all authority in heaven and on earth has been given to him. Then he sends them out to "make disciples of all nations," baptizing the believers and teaching those who are baptized to obey all that he has commanded, and promises to be with them until the end of the age. Even after Jesus' departure, his teaching ministry should continue, so the disciples are charged with the mission to make disciples for him.

Telling Jesus' life story in three parts according to chronological and geographical principles, while organizing his teachings thematically, Matthew follows the literary conventions of ancient biography for classical heroes and philosophers. These accounts also consisted of three main sections: the hero's origins and youth, his accomplishments and public career, and his death and lasting significance. In Greco-Roman culture, Plutarch's *Lives of the Roman Emperors* is the best-known example of biographies that tell the stories of famous and influential emperors, generals, and philosophers, to showcase their virtues of courage, sacrifice, and wisdom. Similarly in Jewish literature, the lives of beloved patriarchs and prophets, such as Abraham, Joseph, Moses, David, Isaiah, and Jeremiah were also intended to demonstrate their qualities of faithfulness, righteousness, and piety and to offer exemplary models for imitation. The three-fold structure of Matthew's gospel indicates that Matthew has transformed the Christian teaching and preaching he found in Mark into a classical biography of Jesus.

The three-fold structure of Matthew's gospel indicates that Matthew has transformed the Christian teaching and preaching he found in Mark into a classical biography of Jesus.

Ancient biography is meant to inform and instruct the reader. By adopting this literary genre, Matthew reveals two of his main purposes. First, he wanted his readers to know Jesus more fully, beyond his redemptive mission as the crucified Messiah that Mark had professed. Why should people believe Jesus was the Messiah or the Son of God, if he could not save himself from the cross? What did he say about the kingdom of God, the final judgment, and the new way of life? How could his followers live together as a church without his physical presence? Providing data concerning Jesus' lineage from David, his authority to perform miracles and forgive sins, his remarkable knowledge of God's will, and his self-sacrifice on the cross, Matthew hoped to strengthen his readers' faith in and commitment to Jesus as the Messiah and the Son of God (16:16). Second, he wanted to *inspire* his readers to adore Jesus so much that they would emulate his love for people and his obedience to God. Imitating Jesus would then enhance their spiritual character. By making Jesus' teaching easily accessible in five discourses, Matthew also made his gospel into a convenient *enchiridion*, or manual, for catechism, a textbook for forming new believers into true disciples of Jesus.

In short, Matthew's main purpose is to help his readers know and believe in Jesus Christ, as the other gospel authors did, and to be inspired and trained to become disciples of Jesus, as clearly scripted in the Great Commission: "Go therefore and make disciples of all nations" (28:19). To be transformed into true disciples of Jesus, therefore, the readers of this gospel need to first know and believe that Jesus is a credible teacher from God. That is why Matthew tells stories to demonstrate Jesus' divine commission as the Messiah and his divine identity as the Son of God with privy knowledge of divine mystery. The readers will learn well if they love and trust their teacher, so Matthew also portrays Jesus' compassion and obedience and preserves his major teachings. Featuring Jesus as a supreme teacher of divine will for the end-time, Matthew is saying to his readers that faith in Jesus Christ and receiving baptism are necessary but not sufficient. It is by doing *righteousness* as Jesus has commanded that baptized believers become true disciples.

Who Were Matthew's First Readers?

Why did Matthew think it is important not only to inspire his readers to believe in Jesus, but also to instruct them to become true disciples of Jesus? We often talk about the same matter in different ways to different audiences. To little children we may speak with simple words and plain ideas; in conversation with grown-ups on formal occasions, we will polish our style. In debate with experts on professional subjects, we employ technical terminology, while with non-professionals we use direct talk when explaining something practical. Who then were Matthew's first readers?

Matthew does not mention his intended readers, their location, or issues of concern, as Paul often does in his letters to the early Christian communities. We may, however, find some clues and hints in the way Matthew tells the story of Jesus and his disciples to acquire a sketch or profile of his audience. To begin with, many of his intended readers were Jewish. The genealogy that links Jesus to Abraham the Jewish patriarch and David the messianic king, the quotations from the Hebrew scriptures that claim to have fulfilled the messianic prophecies, and the nativity stories that are reminiscent of the life of Moses are materials unique to Matthew. These reflect the author's Jewish background; these materials also appealed best to Jewish readers who were familiar with the Hebrew scriptures and believed in their authority. The legal debates over purities and divorce between Jesus and the Pharisees are practical issues that also concerned Jewish readers much more than Gentile ones. Thus we can assume that many of Matthew's readers were Jewish in terms of ethnic and cultural background.

Matthew also wished to reach out to Gentile readers, and it is one reason he considered it necessary to translate simple Semitic words into Greek, such as *Emmanuel* (1:23), *Golgotha* (27:33), and *Eli, Eli, lema sabachthani* (27:46). The final judgment, where all nations will be sorted out like sheep or goats, and the Great Commission to turn all nations into disciples, would speak directly to the Gentile readers too. So it is safe to assume that Matthew's church was a mixed community—ethnically, linguistically, and culturally.

Matthew's readers seemed to be urban inhabitants, as indicated by Matthew's use of the term "city" twenty-six times in his gospel compared to only six in Mark. Some of them might have been well-to-do, as indicated by his copious use of such words as "silver," "gold," and "talent." Given the frequent use of scriptural quotations, allusions, echoes, and the relatively sophisticated debates over legal issues, moreover, many readers must have been educated and possessed of a strong interest in the Jewish law in order to appreciate Matthew's multilayered and sometimes complex arguments. In other words, Matthew's church was far from being a secluded or sectarian group living at the fringe of society.

Most striking in Matthew, however, is the intense hostility he describes between Jesus and the Pharisees in the narrative. To name just a few episodes in the story as example, Jesus

> *Most striking in Matthew is the intense hostility he describes between Jesus and the Pharisees in the narrative.*

bluntly says to the chief priests and the elders that the kingdom of heaven will be "taken away" from them and "given to a people that produces the fruits of the kingdom" (21:43). He also publicly condemns the Pharisees and the scribes, who were well-respected teachers of the law, as self-indulgent hypocrites and murderers (23:13–36). In return, various groups of leaders in Jerusalem combine forces to entrap Jesus and conspire to have him killed: "The Pharisees went out and conspired against him, how to destroy him" (12:14). Although traditional rivals, the Pharisees and the Sadducees, joined hands in rejecting Jesus. The narrator even refers to the synagogue as "theirs"—"Beware of them, for they will hand you over to councils and flog you in their synagogues" (10:17)—as if Jesus had no connection with it whatsoever. All these signs of hostility reflect the wide psychological distance and perhaps social separation that existed between Matthew's church and the Jewish community nearby.

The intense hostility also suggests that Matthew's church was probably located in or near a major city where both Christian community and Jewish synagogue were big and strong enough to be independent from and in contention with each other. Even though scholars have made several proposals, such as Pella, Caesarea, or Sepphoris, the city of Antioch on the Orontes River in Roman Syria remains the most probable location. There are three good reasons for this. In the first place, Ignatius, bishop of Antioch, cited several references and sayings of Jesus in his letters that are found only in Matthew. For instance, Jesus' baptism is meant to "fulfill the righteousness" (Letter to the Smyrnaeans 1:1, found in Matthew 3:15), and false prophets are like wolves wearing sheep's clothing (Letter to the Philadelphians 2:2, found in Matthew 7:15). These letters were written on Ignatius' way to martyrdom in Rome early in the second century, and they are the earliest testimonies to the existence and influence of Matthew's gospel.

As early as 50 CE, moreover, a church was established in Antioch soon after the earliest church in Jerusalem was persecuted by the Jewish authorities and its members were forced to disperse. Some followers of Jesus moved north to Antioch and began to convert both Jews and Gentiles. Barnabas and Paul became their first pastors, and it was there Jesus' followers were first called "Christians" (Acts 11:26). Finally, during and after the First Jewish War (66–70 CE), a great number of Jewish refugees fled to Antioch, the big city north of Palestine, where a significant Jewish community could provide shelter and care for the refugees. There the Pharisaic rabbis quickly assumed leadership in the synagogue after the war.

Consequently, if Matthew's gospel was indeed written in Antioch or its vicinity after 70 CE, several debates that took place there earlier, such as the controversy over table fellowship between the Jewish Christians and the Gentile Christians that triggered a public squabble between Peter and Paul (Galatians 2:11–14) and the Spirit-guided mission to bring the gospel to Asia Minor (Acts 13:1–3), should be considered as part of the heritage of Matthew and his church when he wrote his gospel. It is possible, for instance, that Matthew was making a reference to the apostle Paul, who preached justification by grace, or his radical followers who considered the Jewish law obsolete, when he reported Jesus saying "Whoever breaks one of the least of these commandments, and teaches others to do the same, will be called least in the kingdom of heaven" (5:19). Given the history of the tension over the status of the Jewish and Gentile members in the church at the time of Paul and Peter, along with contemporary groups that may claim

Matthew may have attempted to validate the status of both Jewish and Gentile members in the church by recording two historical commissions that Jesus had made.

those two apostolic traditions, Matthew may have attempted to validate the status of both Jewish and Gentile members in the church by recording two historical commissions that Jesus had made, sending his disciples first to the "lost sheep of the house of Israel" (10:6) and then to "all nations" (28:19).

What Was Matthew's Purpose and Goal?

The ethnic mixture, urban setting, religious tensions, and theological debates described above are part and parcel of the reality of Matthew's community. In addition, there are three urgent issues that we can detect in Matthew's editorial "asides," theological tendencies, and recurrent themes. These were problems that seemed to have been threatening the faith and life of his church, and it is partly to address these urgent concerns that he wrote his gospel. These were spiritual (ignoring the practice of righteousness, complacency over the delay of the *parousia*), polemical (debates with the rabbis, tensions with the synagogue), and pastoral (hypocrisy of the leaders, dissension among members).

First, spiritual issues. In Matthew's gospel Jesus declares at the outset of his ministry that he has "come not to abolish but to fulfill" the law and the prophets, which will never pass away until all is accomplished (5:17). Those who obey the law and teach others to do so will be greatly rewarded (5:19) and those who "practice lawlessness" will be turned away from the kingdom of heaven (7:23). When a rich young man asks Jesus what he should do in order to have eternal life, Jesus says that to enter into life he should "keep the commandments" (19:17) and, if he wants to be perfect, he should also sell all his possessions to help the poor and follow Jesus. Jesus also announces that one who wishes to enter the kingdom of heaven should do righteousness exceeding that of the Pharisees and the scribes because the kingdom of heaven will be taken away from the wicked tenants and given to those who "produces the fruits of the kingdom" (21:43). Righteousness is essential above all: Jesus wants his disciples to observe the teachings of the Pharisees but not to do as they do, "for they do not practice what they teach" (23:3).

These repeated emphases on the importance of following the law, obeying the commandments, and doing righteousness suggest that a significant number of Matthew's readers might have fallen into moral laxity, mistakenly thinking that faith alone will save them. Some readers seem to have also ignored Jesus' promised return to render final judgment, so Matthew accentuated the eschatological warning throughout the gospel in order to call for spiritual vigilance. At the end of each discourse, for instance, Jesus always concludes his teaching by issuing a warning about the final judgment. In the parable of the wedding banquet, for example, a man without a wedding robe is bound and thrown into the outer darkness by the king, even though he has been invited to the feast unexpectedly (22:13). This story ending is a vivid illustration of the message that many are called but few are chosen, and a stern warning for Matthew's readers to live lives worthy of God's grace. He then dedicated the final discourse exclusively to eschatological themes with the "little apocalypse" telling the signs of the end, the coming of the Son of Man, and the parables of the faithful or unfaithful slave, the ten bridesmaids, the talents, and the sheep and the goats. Finally, the gospel ends with Jesus' promise to be always present with his disciples on their mission to make disciples of all nations "to the end of the age" (28:20). Heeding and doing Jesus' teaching will prepare them well for the final judgment. Highlighting Jesus' teaching role, thus, Matthew meant to wake his readers up from their moral and spiritual complacency.

Second, there are polemical issues. Matthew's church was fiercely debating with the rabbis over Jesus' credibility as the Messiah and Son of God and over his church's legitimacy as God's new creation. How do we know that? First to be noted is that Matthew singled out the Pharisees as Jesus' archenemies. They censure Jesus for his association with tax collectors and sinners (9:11); accuse him of sorcery, casting out demons by the power of Beelzebub (9:34; 10:25; 12:24); and call him "impostor" (27:63). With these negative labels, they try to mark Jesus as a rebellious and delinquent leader who deserves to be eliminated. The spotlight on the Pharisees as Jesus' chief foes may also reflect the fact that the rabbis from Yavneh were leading the attack against Matthew's church. After the First Jewish War, the Pharisaic rabbis rose to become the leaders of the Jewish community while the

The spotlight on the Pharisees as Jesus' chief foes may also reflect the fact that the rabbis from Yavneh were leading the attack against Matthew's church.

priests and the Sadducees lost their social functions and leadership positions. In their efforts to rebuild civil order and religious life, the rabbis insisted on keeping the law as they interpreted it. Replacing sacrifice in the Temple, studying the law was now considered a pious act of worship and the only way to national redemption. From the rabbis' point of view, Matthew's church was a heretic sect that taught a perverted version of Judaism. Christians desecrated the Jewish faith in the one true and living God when they confessed Jesus to be the Son of God. They also violated the sacred tradition when they broke the Sabbath law and ignored the purity laws, including those times when Jews and Gentiles sat and ate together in the church.

It was in order to refute the rabbis' charge of "lawlessness" against Christians that Matthew's Jesus solemnly declares that he has not come to destroy the law and the prophets, but to fulfill them, and then delivers six statements based on a pattern of thesis and antithesis: "You have heard that it was said to those of ancient times, 'You shall not murder'; and 'whoever murders shall be liable to judgment.' But I say to you that if you are angry with a brother or sister, you will be liable to judgment" (5:21–22). By this rhetorical device Matthew was attempting to prove that Christians held to a higher standard of the law. In order to reinforce his audience's confidence, moreover, Matthew also portrayed Jesus as a wise teacher of the law who outwits his opponents and silences the Pharisees in a series of entrapping questions and stunning answers (22:15–46).

Finally, it is to countercharge the rabbis that Matthew's Jesus lashes out in relentless indignation against the Pharisees and the scribes enlisting their hypocrisy and wickedness in the six woes: "But woe to you, scribes and Pharisees, hypocrites! For you lock people out of the kingdom of heaven. For you do not go in yourselves, and when others are going in, you stop them" (23:13–14). The gospel even portrays the synagogues as the locus of violence against Jesus' followers. In his mission discourse, for instance, Jesus says to the disciples:

> See, I am sending you out like sheep into the midst of wolves; so be wise as serpents and innocent as doves. Beware of them, for they will hand you over to councils and flog you in their synagogues; and you will be dragged before governors and kings because of me, as a testimony to them and the Gentiles. (10:16–18)

The Jewish leaders are compared to hungry wolves who will hurt Jesus' followers and torture them in their synagogues. Speaking against the Pharisees and the scribes, Jesus also says:

> Therefore I send you prophets, sages, and scribes, some of whom you will kill and crucify, and some you will flog in your synagogues and pursue from town to town, so that upon you may come all the righteous blood shed on earth. (23:34–35)

To encourage his church to hold firm to faith, therefore, Jesus addresses his disciples directly in the ninth beatitude: "Blessed are you when people revile you and persecute you and utter all kinds of evil against you falsely on my account. Rejoice and be glad, for your reward is great in heaven, for in the same way they persecuted the prophets who were before you" (5:11). Facing the rabbis' accusations and the synagogue's harassment, one of Matthew's goals in portraying Jesus as the Christ, the Son of God, and the authoritative teacher was thus to bolster his readers' faith and their understanding of Jesus to withstand the challenges of a hostile Jewish community.

Third, there are pastoral issues. Matthew was also concerned about the quality of leadership in his church and the dissension that threatened his community. For him, the most important task of church leaders was obeying and teaching others to obey Jesus' commandments, which fulfilled the law and the prophets. Doing God's will is the first leadership trait; a good leader teaches by personal example and not by empty words. Thus, Jesus warns his disciples that not all who call him "Lord, Lord" can enter the kingdom of God even if they have prophesied, cast out demons, or performed miracles in his name, but those who do the will of God (7:21–23). While chastising the Pharisees for their love of vainglory, he also turns to the crowds and the disciples, saying: "Therefore, do what they teach you and follow it, but do not do as they do, for they do not practice what they teach" (23:3). A good leader should also be humble, as pride is the greatest lure from Satan, as indicated in the last temptation of Jesus in the wilderness. Over against the Pharisees, therefore, Jesus sternly commands the disciples: "But you are not to be called rabbi, for you have one teacher, . . . Nor are you to be called instructors, for you have one instructor, the Messiah" (23:8, 10). Humility is of paramount importance in good leadership.

Besides the problem of exemplary leadership, Matthew was also worried about the dissension that was tearing his community apart, as indicated by his repeated advice on forgiving one another. In the first antithesis, for instance, Jesus says that his followers should not get angry with a brother or sister lest they commit the sin of murder, should not call one another bad names, and should seek reconciliation before offering gifts at the altar. To drive home the importance of mutual forgiveness, Matthew added a warning to the Lord's Prayer: "For if you forgive others their trespasses, your heavenly Father will also forgive you; but if you do not forgive others, neither will your Father forgive your trespasses" (6:14–15). The best evidence of community infighting can be found in Matthew 18, where Jesus teaches the disciples how to discipline those members who refuse to repent of their sins against others. Sinners should be given due process and be excommunicated only after the entire community has reached a consensus. Peter's subsequent question, "Lord, if another member of the church sins against me, how often should I forgive?" (v. 21) along with the parable of the unforgiving servant, show how earnestly Matthew urged his readers to forgive one another and seek reconciliation so that the church may be united. It is to address these pastoral issues that Matthew included many pertinent teachings of Jesus in the gospel that would help to build up his church.

Matthew's gospel was favorably received because it included a comprehensive story of Jesus' life and a rich compendium of his teaching.

Matthew's gospel began to be widely circulated in the earliest churches soon after its appearance. It was favorably received because it included a comprehensive story of Jesus' life and a rich compendium of his teaching, serving the church well as a foundational text for catechism, worship, and mission. It became the gospel of the church, and for centuries was used as the lectionary text for Sunday worship. As a result, it has a long and complex history of interpretation. Theologians such as Chrysostom, Augustine, and Calvin have all left behind an extensive series of commentaries and sermons on its text and theological message. Matthew's influence on the faith and practice of the church and on the life and history of Western societies is thus deep and wide. For example, the story of the wise men traveling from the East to worship the infant Jesus in Bethlehem serves to enrich the church's Christmas season and promote its missionary efforts to many remote areas of the world. The Sermon on the Mount has done much to shape the moral principles of Christian ethics and triggered major debates on political theories of social justice and just war. Parables like the sheep and the goats have inspired numerous social ministries, charities, and volunteerism in the church.

Unfortunately, Matthew's gospel has also been misinterpreted or misused to cause regrettable damages to the church and the world. For instance, the series of "woes" uttered by Jesus against the Pharisees in Matthew 23 and the curse of Jesus' blood ("His blood be on us and on our children!" 27:25) have been used to justify and endorse anti-Semitism throughout the centuries, while the debate over Peter the apostle as the founder of the Christian church has exacerbated conflict between Roman Catholics and Protestants.

In view of the human catastrophes caused by ethnic discrimination and religious wars, how we decide to parse the polemical language of Matthew's gospel in its own context and to interpret its gospel of salvation for all nations raises important hermeneutical and ethical questions we cannot afford to ignore. Matthew has given us a new gospel, a powerful story of Jesus' life and teaching that can change the world, but it needs to be carefully studied with critical appreciation and prayerful reflection. To that task we will now turn.

CHAPTER TWO

Jesus, the Son of God

In Christian art and tradition the four gospels are often associated with four symbols, the four "living creatures" surrounding the throne of God in the book of Revelation, and represented by a human being, a lion, an ox, and an eagle. Irenaeus and Jerome compared Matthew's gospel to a winged man, perhaps an angel, while Augustine compared it to a lion. The use of different symbols for the four canonical gospels indicates that the early theologians of the church understood that each gospel has a distinctive view of Jesus and each highlights a particular aspect of his character. It is only by reading all four gospels that one can grasp the multiple aspects of Jesus' identity and role, and through his life, death, and resurrection to gain a glimpse of the mystery of God. Human or lion, it remains a mere symbol. So we ask: what do those two symbols really say about Jesus in Matthew's gospel? Who is Jesus and what does he do? How can Matthew's story of Jesus transform the belief and life of those who encounter it?

As we discussed in the last chapter, ancient biography often began with background reports about the origins and youth of the hero. Why was such background information important? First of all, ancient readers were curious about the hero's family lineage and educational preparation, assuming that those of outstanding accomplishments must be qualitatively different from ordinary people by nature and by nurture. Most readers also wanted to find out the reasons why their heroes were so much braver or wiser than ordinary people; to be capable of such extraordinary achievements, would they not have divine connections and special upbringing that was out of the ordinary? The unusual signs and events that were reported to take place at their births, and the exceptional teachers with whom they studied, were the best indications of divine favor. For Jewish and Christian biographies, fulfillment of prophecies from the scriptures was also significant—it meant the hero's accomplishment was predestined and commissioned by God. The beginning section of an ancient biography, therefore, usually performed two important functions: to prove the hero's divine favor and to introduce his uncommon qualities. Such background information explained why the hero could achieve so much in life, as well as divulging the biographer's own point of view on the hero.

In the first part of his gospel, stories of Jesus' birth and infancy, Matthew highlights two special titles—Messiah and Son of God—to introduce Jesus as intimately related to the divine. The use of these titles prepares Matthew's readers to better understand what lay behind Jesus' public ministry of healing and teaching as well as the significance of his redemptive death. These two honorific titles indicate Jesus' divine commission from, and unique relationship with, God. They also explain from where his authority and mission originate.

Messiah

Matthew begins his gospel with a genealogy of "Jesus the Messiah" and calls Jesus "Messiah" later on, a title that means "the anointed one" in Hebrew. There were many Jewish men named "Jesus"—*Yeshuah,* or "Joshua" in Hebrew—meaning "God saves." There were also several "messiahs" in Jewish history, such as Aaron the priest, David the king of Judah, and the Persian king Cyrus, all of whom were anointed by God to carry out remarkable acts of salvation for God's people. By all accounts King David was the messiah *par excel-*

lence, a favored servant of the Lord and the most celebrated king of Israel, who built and ruled over a powerful kingdom. The Israelites looked for the coming of another Davidic messiah. Before Jesus' time, a small remnant of the nation of Judah had returned from exile in Babylon and rebuilt the Second Temple in Jerusalem, but the Jewish people continued to suffer heavy taxation and brutal oppression under the rule of the Romans. They longed for freedom and prosperity, and eagerly waited for a mighty messiah of the Lord, someone like King David, to rescue them from the tyranny of their oppressors and political overlords. The act of waiting for the Messiah thus became both a political hope and a religious prayer.

The act of waiting for the Messiah thus became both a political hope and a religious prayer.

In view of such popular expectation, Matthew is extremely audacious to claim that Jesus of Nazareth is the Messiah. It is true that Jesus earned a reputation as an outspoken prophet and compassionate miracle worker among the poor peasants in Galilee, but in the end he was arrested, humiliated, and executed by Pontius Pilate, the Roman governor in Judea. If Jesus could not save himself from the suffering and death of a criminal on the cross, how could he have been the Messiah? If he could not summon God's angels to fight his torturers and executors, how could believers rely on him to win liberation from oppression? What happened to Jesus in Jerusalem simply did not match people's hope for the Messiah, who was to come as a mighty savior (21:9). The immediate question for Matthew's earliest readers, therefore, was—how can Jesus be the Messiah?

It is precisely to answer such a question that Matthew begins his gospel with Jesus' genealogy. Jewish people believe that the Messiah has to be an offspring of David, because it is to David and his descendants that God promised to confer the ruling power of the throne forever: "Your house and your kingdom shall be made sure forever before me; your throne shall be established forever" (2 Sam. 7:16). The first point Matthew has to prove, therefore, is that Jesus is truly the offspring of David, and his first piece of evidence is Joseph's genealogy in David's family line. Even though Jesus was not physically born from Joseph, the Jewish law allows him, an adopted son, to be a legal heir to Joseph and thereby a legitimate offspring of

David. For this reason, it is significant that Joseph gave Jesus his name as a legal act of adoption. By tracing Jesus' lineage further back to Abraham, the Jewish patriarch through whom all nations will be blessed, Matthew intimates that Jesus is not only the Messiah of the Jews but also a blessing to the Gentiles.

That Jesus is the awaited Messiah is underscored again in the story of the magi from the East who traveled to Jerusalem to search for the newborn king in order to worship him: "Where is the child who has been born king of the Jews? For we observed his star at its rising, and have come to pay him homage" (2:2). The chief priests and the scribes were able to discover from the scriptures that Bethlehem was the birthplace of the Messiah, as prophesied by the prophet Micah, but they did not care enough to go there to worship him. Perhaps these religious leaders did not really want a "shepherd of Israel" to rise up and share their ruling authority, an issue that would come up directly when Jesus arrived in Jerusalem. They challenged the adult Jesus with a blunt question: "By what authority are you doing these things?" (21:23). So it is ironic to see that while King Herod and Jewish leaders rejected Jesus, the wise men from the East honored him as the Messiah. This stark contrast suggests that God is impartial, who grants divine truth to all peoples. Jesus the Messiah will be a savior to both the Jews and the Gentiles. Sadly, however, human desire for power turns some people against him.

In the long middle section of the gospel, which focuses on Jesus' teaching and healing career in Galilee, Matthew tells a few more stories to underscore Jesus' messianic identity. One instance involves John the Baptist, who was imprisoned because of his harsh criticism of the incestuous marriage of Herod Antipas, son of King Herod. Having heard about Jesus' ministry, John sent his disciples to ask Jesus whether he was the Messiah. In reply, Jesus called his attention to the messianic works he had done to make the blind see, the lame walk, the lepers clean, the deaf hear, the dead raised, and the poor hear the good news (11:4–6). His works of wonder and healing had demonstrated his messianic power and proved his identity beyond any doubt, if only people were willing to see.

The most revealing event of Jesus' true identity takes place when Jesus traveled with his disciples through Caesarea Philippi and asked his disciples, "Who do you say that I am?" When Peter replied, "You are the Messiah, the Son of the living God" (16:16), Jesus joyfully confirmed his confession as a divine revelation and granted him the keys of the kingdom of heaven. Later on, after they have reached Jerusalem, Jesus asked his opponents the Pharisees to explain why David called the Messiah his Lord in Psalm 110, if the Messiah is indeed a son of David: "The LORD says to my lord: 'Sit at my right hand until I make your enemies your footstool'" (v. 1). "The LORD" in the sentence refers to God, and "my lord" refers to the Messiah who will be exalted to a position of authority on God's side. Since "my lord" (*Adonai* in Hebrew) is a title usually reserved for the almighty God, calling the Messiah "my lord" is to pledge loyalty to the Messiah who will enjoy the honor with God after winning the victory over all enemies. So who is greater, David or the Messiah? In this diatribe, Jesus referred to himself as the Messiah who will be exalted to divine lordship, sharing glory with God.

Since Jesus has been confirmed as the Messiah in the gospel narrative, it is ironic for the reader to hear the high priest demanding that Jesus answer under oath whether he was the Messiah during his trial by the council (26:63), and equally so that the Roman governor orders a plate hung on the cross with the verdict "This is Jesus, the King of the Jews!" in several languages (27:37).

Through genealogy and several episodes in the narrative, therefore, Matthew has evidently tried to establish Jesus' credentials as the Messiah. Jesus is the king of the Jews who was born to carry out the works of salvation for God's people. He did not dispatch a host of angels to crush human enemies, but he cured diseases and expelled demons with divine power. He then died a sacrificial death to forgive sins, and triumphantly rose from the grave to conquer death. In Matthew's view, Jesus is the Messiah who has gone beyond popular expectation to demonstrate how God's promise to save the people has been mightily fulfilled.

Son of God

Matthew also claims that Jesus is the Son of God, a title signifying a unique and intimate relationship with God. For the Jews, this title was not only presumptuous, but blasphemous—they believed the almighty God is the holy creator of the world, while human beings are nothing but sinful creatures in need of mercy. For both theological reasons and reasons of religious piety, the clear boundary between God and humans cannot be transgressed. It is not surprising, therefore, that Jesus was immediately condemned to death by the high priest, when he admitted to be both Messiah and *the Son of God* during the trial. Offensive as it may have been to the Jews, this title is key to the Christology of Matthew's church. It is part of Peter's confession at Caesarea Philippi, "You are the Messiah, the Son of the living God," on which rock Jesus would build his church (16:18). Its importance to Matthew is evident when Peter's confession is compared to its parallel in Mark, which simply states, "You are the Messiah" (Mark 8:29).

For the Gentiles, steeped in Hellenistic culture, the title "Son of God" gave them no difficulties at all. Great heroes were often called "sons of god" to indicate their privileged relationship with the divine world, and that privileged relationship is the reason why they were endowed with exceptional qualities and superhuman powers that brought about their miraculous achievements. Around the time of Jesus, moreover, the term "son of God" (*Divi filius*) was used to honor several Roman emperors. After Julius Caesar was assassinated, for example, the Senate honored him as a divine being taken up into heaven (*apotheosis*), and as a result, his adopted son Octavian Augustus became "son of God." When Augustus died, he was also deified and his adopted son Tiberius came to be called "son of the divine Augustus." Even though these Roman emperors were not widely worshipped apart for the imperial cult in western Asia Minor, this title recognizes their divine connections and political contributions.

> For the Gentiles, steeped in Hellenistic culture, the title "Son of God" gave them no difficulties at all.

For Matthew, however, Jesus is qualitatively different from other sons of God in Greco-Roman culture, as indicated by his use of the word "living" to describe God in Peter's confession, where he calls Jesus "the Son of the *living God*." Matthew is careful to distinguish Jesus' God from the pagan gods, insisting that God is the only true God who created the world and reigns in history. Since Jesus is the son of this true and living God, he is not "son of god" in a metaphorical or political sense; more than an extraordinary person, he has a unique status and intimate relationship with the true and living God. That gives him unprecedented access to God's mystery and thus the authority to reveal God's will. Hence, he is the Son of God.

Given that his audience included Jewish readers who considered the "Son of God" a blasphemous title, along with Gentile readers who understood it metaphorically, how does Matthew argue for Jesus to be the Son of the living God? The way he navigates these turbulent theological waters is remarkable. First and foremost, Matthew appeals to direct revelation from God to validate Jesus' identity as the Son of God. The first time Jesus was identified that way was shortly before his birth, when an angel of the Lord appeared to Joseph and persuaded him to marry Mary by reassuring him that she became pregnant by the Holy Spirit. Matthew emphasizes that Joseph did not have any sexual relationship with Mary before Jesus was born in order to underscore Jesus' unusual birth. Then God affirmed Jesus' identity and sonship in an epiphany when he came up from the water after baptism. The heavens opened, the Spirit of God descended on Jesus like a dove, and a voice from heaven declared: "This is my Son, the Beloved, with whom I am well pleased" (3:17). God made the same declaration again to Jesus and his three beloved disciples on the mountain of transfiguration (17:5).

Jesus' major opponents also functioned as foils strengthening Jesus' identity as the Son of God. In the temptation story, for instance, the devil's repeated challenge to Jesus: "If you are the Son of God . . ." inadvertently reflects his acknowledgment of Jesus' status as the Son of God. The devil recognized Jesus' divine status, but as part of his rebellion against God wanted to trick Jesus to behave unworthily and degrade that honorable title. The same irony can be seen in the high priest's interrogation of Jesus at his trial. The high priest might have an inkling of Jesus' divine power as demonstrated in the miracles but did not wish to admit it. So he convicted Jesus of blasphemy as soon as Jesus admitted to be the Messiah and the Son of God. Finally, the Roman centurion presiding over Jesus' crucifixion was so terrified by the earthquake and other natural portents at Jesus' death that he shouted: "Truly this man was God's son!" (27:54).

But most noteworthy of all is Jesus' self-revelation in the lonely moment when he was lamenting over the cities of Galilee that rejected him despite his many miracles. After thanking God for hiding the secrets of the kingdom of heaven from the wise and revealing them to the infants, he declared: "All things have been handed over to me by my Father; and no one knows the Son except the Father, and no one knows the Father except the Son, and anyone to whom the Son chooses to reveal him" (11:27).

This declaration shows that Jesus regarded himself as the Son of God who enjoyed a unique relationship with God and exclusive knowledge of God's secrets. Except through Jesus no one can understand God, and only those whom he has chosen will be able to receive revelation. Confessing Jesus to be the Son of God means to honor his divine status as the Son, his intimate relationship with God, and his inmost knowledge of God's will. Here lies a fundamental difference between the Christian view of the Son of God and that of Jewish or Gentile.

Teacher of God's Will

With these two titles, Messiah and Son of God, Matthew answers the important question of Jesus' identity, but it should be noted that these titles were also commonly used by early Christian writers. Does Matthew have any additional insights to share? I will argue that he does highlight a special role of Jesus that is timely for Matthew's own church and equally important to Christians today—that of an authoritative teacher of God's will with deep eschatological significance. This christological role answers the question regarding what Jesus does and yields some clues to the purposes of Matthew's gospel.

Matthew highlights Jesus' teaching role by choosing and arranging several stories of Jesus' birth and youth to recall the well-known stories of Moses.

What kind of teacher was Jesus? Matthew gets his point across by arranging his materials and characterizing Jesus in special ways. At the outset, Matthew highlights Jesus' teaching role by choosing several stories of Jesus' birth and youth to recall the well-known stories of Moses in the Hebrew scriptures. In the infancy narratives he records that all children of the age of two and under in Bethlehem were massacred by Herod, but Jesus was protected by God and his parents fled into Egypt. These episodes evoke the familiar stories of the Hebrew infants who were slaughtered by Pharaoh, the baby Moses who was rescued by Pharaoh's daughter, and his departure from Egypt.

Later, after becoming an adult, Jesus emerged from the water of the Jordan River after baptism and resisted the temptations of the devil in the wilderness for forty days. These two episodes echo the famous stories of Moses leading the Israelites through the waters of the Red Sea and their temptations in the desert for forty years. In Matthew 5, the gospel describes how Jesus went up to a mountaintop to teach the Sermon on the Mount, reminiscent of the legendary story of Moses' ascent to Mount Sinai to receive the Ten Commandments. These parallel stories strongly suggest that Jesus is the new Moses and, like Moses, he will be the savior and law-giver of God's new people. These parallel stories show that to save his people from their sins, Jesus would assume the role of teacher and rabbi to inform the Israelites of God's demands so that they know how to live a life of righteousness. He will also play a redemptive role in dying as the crucified Messiah so that his people's sins may be forgiven. Thus Jesus' mission is twofold—to reveal God's will and to demonstrate God's love.

It is worth noting that Matthew frames Jesus' ministry in Galilee with two summary reports that mention three tasks, "teaching in their synagogues, and proclaiming the good news of the kingdom, and curing every diseases and every sickness" (4:23, 9:35). Teaching is listed as Jesus' number one task. In comparison, when we look at their parallels in Mark, we find that Mark mentions only two tasks— "proclaiming the message in their synagogues and casting out demons" (Mark 1:39). Even though Mark tells us that the crowds were "amazed" by Jesus' new teaching with authority, his gospel does not report on Jesus' teachings nearly as much as his miracles. Evidently, then, Matthew is convinced that teaching God's will is a priority of Jesus' ministry. There is no wonder that Jesus' first public act in Matthew's gospel is delivering the Sermon on the Mount with great authority before his disciples and a big crowd.

Most remarkable are the five teaching discourses that are used to frame and structure the narrative of Jesus' public career from Galilee to Jerusalem.

If we look on Jesus as a new Moses with teaching authority, we will see that Jesus starts his celebrated ministry with the Sermon on the Mount in Galilee and ends with the parables of the final judgment in Jerusalem. Three other discourses are inserted in the middle portion: mission instructions to Jewish towns in chapter 10, parables of the kingdom of heaven in chapter 13, and advices on community life in chapter 18. At the end of each discourse, the narrator repeatedly says, "When Jesus had finished saying . . ." he went on to do something else, as if teaching was more important than healing the sick, debating the Pharisees, or other activities. Furthermore it is significant to note that, at the end of the last discourse, the narrator writes "when Jesus had finished saying all these things . . ." (26:1). Matthew seems to suggest that, after Jesus had taught *all* the important lessons regarding God's will, he was ready to face his sacrificial death in Jerusalem. Given the prominence of the five teaching discourses in the gospel, one scholar has gone so far as to call these five discourses the "New Pentateuch" (five books of Moses) of the Christian church.

In light of Jesus' prominent role as teacher, it makes perfect sense that Matthew would end his gospel with the scene of the Great Commission, in which the risen Jesus sent his disciples out to make disciples of all nations by baptizing them in the name of the Father, of the Son, and of the Holy Spirit, and by teaching them to obey *everything* that he has commanded (28:19–20). The use of the word "everything" in 28:20 recalls an earlier statement: "When Jesus had finished saying all these things, he said to his disciples, 'You know that after two days the Passover is coming, and the Son of Man will be handed over to be crucified'" (26:1–2). By "all" Matthew is probably referring back to all five discourses in the gospel. Jesus' commandments are so vital to God's people that they have to be taught, learned, and obeyed even after his departure. His teaching mission is so important that it shall be carried on by the disciples until the end of the age.

Wise Interpreter of the Law

Who Jesus is and how he behaves as a character interacting with other characters in the gospel story also reflects Matthew's desire to show his prominence as a religious teacher. In four remarkable ways, he is portrayed as a wise interpreter of the law, and indeed a supreme teacher of God's will.

In the first place, Jesus sets a tone for his ministry by declaring that he has come "not to abolish, but to fulfill" the law and the prophets at the beginning of his sermon on the mountaintop. He both teaches and demands a higher standard of righteousness than the traditional teachers do, spelling it out in a series of antithetical sayings that underline the differences between the old standards and the life in the kingdom of heaven—"You have heard that it was said. . . . but I say to you" (5:21–48). He also claims that his words are God's will that should be followed in order to enter the kingdom of heaven on the final day, and there is no wonder that the crowds are astounded by his teaching authority, unrivaled by their scribes: "Now when Jesus had finished saying these things, the crowds were astounded at his teaching" (7:28).

Second, Jesus chooses twelve believers to be his disciples, calling people to take on his yoke of the law and learn from him (11:29). In response to his summons, his disciples give up their jobs and leave their families behind to follow him, learning from his teaching of the law, hearing his proclamation of the kingdom of heaven, and witnessing his powerful miracles. They also receive private explanations from Jesus on the mystery of the parables and a special warning against the influential teaching of the Pharisees and Sadducees—"Jesus said to them, 'Watch out, and beware of the yeast of the Pharisees and Sadducees.'" (16:6). Even though they retreat into hiding after his arrest, the disciples are gathered together to worship the risen Jesus and are commissioned to continue his ministry of making disciples.

Third, Jesus is acknowledged as a religious teacher by other prominent and recognized teachers of the law. Even though they criticize his behavior and disagree with his ideas, all of Jesus' opponents consistently address him as "teacher" while, by contrast, disciples and believers call him "Lord." The only exception is Judas, who calls Jesus "rabbi" when he kisses him and betrays him to the Jewish authorities; the disciple turned traitor who becomes the exception that proves the rule. Jesus is considered a tough rival, so teachers from different groups combine forces to entrap him with controversial questions regarding taxes, resurrection, and the greatest commandment. But Jesus outwits them all, and silences them with a counter-question: if the Messiah is a son of David, he asks, why does David call him "my Lord" in Psalm 110:1 (22:45)?

Finally, Jesus claims an exclusive authority as the only teacher for his disciples. In a saying preserved only in Matthew, Jesus chastises the Pharisees for their arrogance and sternly says to the disciples:

> But you are not to be called rabbi, for you have one teacher, and you are all students. And call no one your father on earth, for you have one Father—the one in heaven. Nor are you to be called instructors, for you have one instructor, the Messiah. (23:8–10)

Because Jesus refers to himself as the Messiah, it is possible that this saying from M source originated from a post-Easter tradition in the early church rather than the historical Jesus. In Matthew's gospel, however, this saying expresses Jesus' assertion that he alone is the teacher of his followers. Matthew uses both Jewish ("rabbi") and Gentile ("instructor") terms to emphasize that the only teacher with the ultimate authority should be Jesus Christ himself. In fact his disciples ought to be wary of the temptation of letting themselves get carried away by honorific titles, be it rabbi, Father, or instructor. It is conceivable that this saying served internally as a warning to the Christian leaders in Matthew's church and externally as a critique against the Pharisaic rabbis in the synagogue.

Why Is Jesus' Teaching Role Important?

Why did Matthew portray Jesus as a supreme teacher? Assuming he wrote the gospel not in vacuum, but with the major issues of his church in mind, the answer lies largely in the social-historical context of the community that made up his audience. Before we try to link Matthew's most urgent concerns with the issues besetting his church, however, four traits of Jesus as teacher are worth further consideration.

Unlike the Jewish rabbis or Greco-Roman philosophers of his time, Jesus was a wandering teacher, an *itinerant*. He did not establish a yeshiva or school in which to sit and teach those who decide to come and learn from him, but traveled from town to town to teach the kingdom of heaven to all people, regardless of their social or economic status. He called twelve disciples to follow him, but did not ask for tuition as the teachers of classical antiquity did. While on the road, he relied on the generosity of friends and strangers who listened to his messages and accepted him as teacher. This itinerancy shows his eagerness to preach the kingdom of heaven and his dedication to teach God's will to everyone freely and tirelessly. He was determined to find and bring the lost sheep of the house of Israel back to God's fold and guide them to live a new life so that they might receive eternal blessings at the final judgment.

> *Unlike the Jewish rabbis or Greco-Roman philosophers of his time, Jesus was a wandering teacher, an itinerant.*

The manner in which Jesus contrasts his new commandment against the traditional law of Moses vividly illustrates his unabashed claim to teaching *authority*. That authority is not missed by the dumbfounded crowds, who find it surpassing that of their scribes (7:28). Jesus' authority to teach the law is immediately matched by his authority to heal a servant of the centurion in Capernaum (8:9) and to forgive the sins of a paralytic (9:6). Thus, Jesus' ministry in Galilee is marked by the extraordinary authority he possesses. As soon as he arrives in Jerusalem, however, it becomes a major source of controversy. The chief priests and the elders ask him by whose authority he teaches and heals (21:23), which then sets off a series of polemical parables (the two sons, the wicked tenants, and the wedding banquet) suggesting that Jesus is the Son of God (21:37; 22:2). With these parables, Jesus intimates that his authority comes from his high status as the Son of God. At the end of the gospel, furthermore, the risen Jesus said to them:

> All authority in heaven and on earth has been given to me. Go therefore and make disciples of all nations, baptizing them in the name of the Father and of the Son and of the Holy Spirit, and teaching them to obey everything that I have commanded you. (28:18–20)

It is by that authority he sends out his disciples to make disciples of all nations. Evidently, Jesus makes a remarkable impression on all people around him—crowds, opponents, and disciples—with his authority to teach and to heal. Even though not everyone can understand it, Matthew's own readers have been informed of Jesus' mission as the Messiah and identity as the Son of God and so they are able to see the origin of his authority.

Jesus' third quality, *wisdom*, is most brilliantly demonstrated in the gospel's controversy stories. For instance, in defense of John the Baptist's ascetic lifestyle and his own friendly association with tax collectors and sinners, Jesus replies, "Yet wisdom is vindicated by her deeds" (11:19). By saying this he is comparing himself to the personification of wisdom in Jewish tradition, especially in the book of Proverbs and the Wisdom of Solomon, who like him has been underrated. Yet in his reply to the tricky question regarding whether to pay taxes to Caesar, Jesus' wisdom is again revealed. His questioners apparently wish him to incriminate himself before the Roman authorities if he says no or to discredit himself before his followers if he says yes. But Jesus outmaneuvers his opponents, saying, "Give therefore to the emperor the things that are the emperor's, and to God the things that are God's" (22:21). This answer saves him from political danger because it does not necessarily dodge the taxes owed to the emperor or slight the offering due to the Temple treasury. It also has religious merit, because it can be interpreted to mean that all things should be offered to God because all things belong to God.

> *Jesus compares himself to the personification of wisdom in Jewish tradition, especially in the book of Proverbs and the Wisdom of Solomon, who like him has been underrated.*

Finally, the literary form of biography makes it possible for Matthew to show how Jesus *models righteousness*. He heals the sick and befriends the outcast, so his actions bear witness to his beatitudes, pronouncing blessings on the vulnerable and to his teaching that God loves mercy more than sacrifice. After an intense night of wrestling with God in the garden of Gethsemane, Jesus willingly submits himself to God's plan for him to die on the cross for all people, including the crowds that betray him: "My Father, if it is possible, let this cup pass from me; yet not what I want, but what you want" (26:39, 42). Again, his action sets a good example for his teaching on loving enemies and his advice to "strive first for the kingdom of God and his righteousness" (6:33). Jesus is a respectable teacher who teaches not simply by words but also by deeds. Disciples can imitate his behavior and obey his commandments.

Why did Matthew depict Jesus as a teacher of God's will who is itinerant, authoritative, wise, and exemplary? I would say that Matthew had three main purposes in doing so, which are didactic, polemical, and pastoral.

First, given the fact that Matthew chose to compose his gospel in the form of biography, his first purpose must be didactic. He wanted to inform his readers of their faith in Jesus and guide them to build character as worthy disciples. By providing significant information about Jesus' background, accomplishments, and legacy, Matthew tried to prove Jesus' special mission as Messiah and divine identity as Son of God so that his readers would know and believe in Jesus as their savior, who was sent by God to deliver them from their sins by teaching them the new life of the kingdom of heaven and by dying for their sins on the cross. To inspire his readers to follow Jesus as Lord, Matthew also showed how Jesus interpreted the law and the prophets with authority, healed the sick with compassion, and faced death as an innocent man with courage. To urge his readers to imitate Jesus, he showed them how Jesus rejected the devil's temptations and obeyed God even unto death. It was to help them become Jesus' disciples, moreover, that Matthew organized Jesus' teachings into five pedagogical discourses. Depicting Jesus as an authoritative teacher certainly supported this didactic purpose.

Matthew's second purpose was polemical in nature. Writing in Antioch in the aftermath of the First Jewish War, he witnessed the fact that the Pharisaic rabbis were consolidating their power by purging dissident groups from Jewish communities. It was a difficult time for both Jews and Christians. The city of Jerusalem and its temple had been destroyed, and the Pharisaic rabbis became the leaders of the Jewish communities. They tried to rebuild Jewish life by teaching their people to obey the Torah as they instructed, while Christians and other groups were condemned as *minim* (heretics) that needed to be challenged and expelled from the synagogues. Christians were therefore compelled to defend their faith in Jesus as the Messiah and to explain to the leaders of the synagogue why they worshipped him as the Son of God. Furthermore, they were often accused of violating the Jewish laws by the rabbis, just as Jesus was accused by the Pharisees. As the church and the synagogue were painfully parting ways, it was Matthew's goal to emphasize Jesus' mission as the Messiah, his identity as the Son of God, and his role as the teacher of God's will to help his readers redefine their faith and rebut the rabbis' challenges. That is why his gospel so often depicts Jesus as wiser than the Pharisees and the scribes; it helped to support his polemic purpose.

> *As the church and the synagogue were painfully parting ways, it was Matthew's goal to emphasize Jesus' mission as the Messiah, his identity as the Son of God, and his role as the teacher of God's will to help his readers redefine their faith.*

Finally, Matthew wrote his gospel with a pastoral purpose in mind. Matthew's church may have been plagued by internal conflict, leadership rivalry, and spiritual crisis, and hence he frequently advised these new Christians to forgive one another, and warned them about both hypocrisy and self-delusion:

> Not everyone who says to me, "Lord, Lord," will enter the kingdom of heaven, but only one who does the will of my Father in heaven. On that day many will say to me, "Lord, Lord, did we not prophesy in your name, and cast out demons in your name, and do many deeds of power in your name?" Then I will declare to them, "I never knew you; go away from me, you evildoers." (7:21–23)

Matthew seemed worried that his multiethnic community might be torn apart, with some weak members being misled and its leaders becoming complacent about the final reckoning before God. With the view to forestalling these crises, he collected and compiled some of Jesus' major teachings in the five discourses so that his readers may learn to obey Jesus' commandments and become faithful disciples.

Shaping the Faith and Life of the Church

By highlighting Jesus as the Messiah, Son of God, and supreme teacher, Matthew hoped to convince his readers to believe firmly in him as their savior from sins, to resist pressure from Pharisaic rabbis, and to avert conflict among church leaders. Obviously, they must be persuaded to accept his Jesus as Lord and be willing to follow Jesus' words and deeds—that is, to become Jesus' disciples—in order for his purposes to be fulfilled. How persuasive is Matthew's portrayal of Jesus? How could his threefold view of Jesus shape the faith and life of his church?

As the Messiah, Jesus heals the sick with compassion and casts out demons with power, a sign that the kingdom of heaven has arrived. As the sick and the possessed are released from the suffering and disease and the bondage of evil powers, the salvation of God becomes manifest in his ministry. Seeing his messianic works, some disciples seem to hope that he will also liberate them politically when he travels to Jerusalem. Against popular expectation, however, Jesus wants to save the world not by overcoming the agents of Roman oppression with military force, but by restoring every lost soul to God the Father through spiritual transformation. His primary concern is to save his people from their sins. That is how the world will be saved, because spiritual transformation has to begin with liberation from sin and reconciliation with God. As soon as Peter confesses Jesus to be the Messiah, therefore, Jesus sternly tells his disciples that he will go to Jerusalem to suffer in the hands of the priests and the elders, and to die on the cross so that people's sins can be forgiven. Jesus' messianic works in performing healing miracles and dying a redemptive death vividly illustrate God's power and love. They also attest to the faithfulness of God who keeps the promises of the prophets and cares for the people. In Jesus the Messiah, Matthew's readers may see that God is their loving Father in heaven who has come near to offer them salvation from sins and many heavenly blessings.

As the Son of God, Jesus has a special revelation of God's mystery and exclusive knowledge of God's plan. He wants everybody to know the will of God the Father, so with open arms he invites everyone who is weary and burdened to come and learn from him, that they may find rest in their souls. To prevent his followers from spiritual and moral complacency, Jesus also issues repeated warnings about the sure coming of the final judgment and announces the high standards by which God will judge the world. In doing so, he reveals to his disciples that God is both just and generous. To uphold justice, God will separate the righteous from the wicked on the day of final reckoning that they may receive rewards or punishments according to their life. This final judgment will surely come, even if it seems delayed. Yet because God is merciful and wants all people to enjoy eternal blessings, God sent the Son to call for repentance and teach people how to live.

The double nature of God as both just and generous is most clearly revealed in the parable of the wicked tenants. It tells the story of a landowner who plants a flourishing vineyard and lets it out to his tenants. Even though these tenants refuse to pay the rent, the landowner sends his servants to remind them again and again. Even as his servants are brutally beaten and killed, the landowner still offers them more and more chances to act righteously toward him and pay what they owe. Finally he takes the risk of sending his own son in hopes that the wicked tenants will honor him and pay their dues, and it is not until his son is killed that the owner finally demands justice to be visited on those wicked tenants: "Therefore I tell you, the kingdom of God will be taken away from you and given to a people that produces the fruits of the kingdom" (21:43). As the Son of God, therefore, Jesus shows that God is both just and generous, and his people are urged to become perfect as their heavenly Father is perfect.

As teacher, Jesus chooses twelve disciples to follow him. They witness his kindness in healing the sick, his love for the despised, and his determination to obey God even if it means suffering and death on the cross. Jesus sets an inspiring example showing them how to love and serve God. The disciples also receive from him insight into the mysteries of the parables and are sent out to preach the kingdom of heaven in cities and towns. All along, Jesus is keen in training them to become faithful and learned disciples. When they are slow to believe in his power, Jesus chastises them—"You of little faith!"—and when they fail to perceive the point of his words, he asks them bluntly: "Are you also still without understanding?" When he condemns the Pharisees for their hypocrisy, he also turns it

When Jesus condemns the Pharisees for their hypocrisy, he also turns it into a teaching moment, immediately admonishing his disciples to avoid those practices.

into a teaching moment, immediately admonishing his disciples to avoid those practices. Moreover, he promises his constant presence with them on their mission to make disciples of all nations. Jesus is a thoughtful and ever-present teacher to his disciples. By imitating his way of life and obeying his commandments, Matthew's readers could also learn what to believe and how to act properly as children of God.

Messiah, Teacher, and Son

We have seen that Matthew presents Jesus as the Messiah, the Son of God, and the supreme teacher to inspire his readers to become faithful disciples. At the end of the first century, his threefold portrayal of Jesus might have helped the church in Antioch address the challenges from the rabbis and the crisis of internal conflict. It also became an important apologetic resource for the early church fathers when they tried to define Christian faith and debate with the Jewish opponents in the second century. In his *Dialogue with Trypho*, for instance, Justin Martyr mentioned that the rabbis of his time had sent emissaries to many places to condemn Jesus as a "Galilean deceiver" and accuse him of teaching a "godless and lawless heresy." In rebuttal, Justin described Christians as people who confessed Jesus to be "Christ, and a teacher from and Son of God" who had risen from the dead. He argued that Christians did not hate the rabbis for conceiving prejudices against them, but would pray for their repentance so that they may obtain mercy from God. Evidently, the three christological titles of Messiah, Teacher, and Son had become a vital foundation of Christian faith, and were used to refute the rabbis' false accusations. As the Messiah and the Son of God, Jesus' mission and identity are godly. As teacher, Jesus' teaching is righteous; he reveals God's will in the law and the prophets.

The image of Jesus as a supreme teacher of God's will with authority, wisdom, and eschatological fervor is particularly prominent in the theology and iconography of the Eastern Orthodox Church, which worships Jesus as "Teacher and *Pantocrator*." This image reminds us that Jesus the supreme teacher has taught us how to live a life worthy of God's grace and ready for the final judgment, and it is by Jesus the enthroned king that the world will be judged.

Through the redemptive death of Jesus the Messiah, our sins have been forgiven. By the grace of Jesus the Son of God, we have become children of God. What we should do, then, is to conduct our life as Jesus the teacher has taught us in words and deeds. We know by experience that we often forget our privileged status as the children of God and turn God's free grace, which was heavily paid by the blood of Christ, into a cheap grace. Our Christian life does not measure up to God's standard. So it is imperative to remember Dietrich Bonhoeffer's exhortation to rededicate our life as faithful disciples of Jesus, willing to pay the cost of discipleship each and every day.

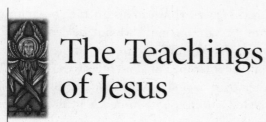

CHAPTER THREE

The Teachings of Jesus

In our society specialized knowledge brings power and prosperity, so young people study hard to become professionals such as doctors, attorneys, and scientists. We also value expert knowledge that sustains our physical and spiritual well-being, so people in crisis would seek guidance from specialists such as trainers, psychologists, and priests. Teachers with specialty and expertise are therefore highly respected. In Jesus' time, people had the same desires for success and happiness, for which they often turned to philosophers or religious leaders for direction. For the Greeks and Romans, there were the Stoics, Epicureans, and Cynics; the teachers of the Jews were the Pharisees, Sadducees, Essenes, and the followers of John the Baptist. Each offered a coherent system of meaning for life and a practical method of training for soul, so each attracted a significant number of followers.

Jesus was an expert teacher, so charismatic and wise that his disciples considered it worthwhile to leave family and livelihood behind in order to follow him. In previous chapters we have seen how extraordinary Jesus was, as Messiah and Son of God; here, we will discover how extraordinary his teaching was. How can his teaching be characterized? At the outset of the Sermon on the Mount, he declares: "For I tell you, unless your righteousness exceeds that of the scribes and Pharisees, you will never enter the kingdom of heaven" (5:20). Urging people to put their trust in God, again Jesus says: "But strive first for the kingdom of God and his righteousness, and all these things will be given to you as well" (6:33). At the conclusion of the parable of the sheep and the goats, those who are condemned will "go away into eternal punishment, but the righteous into eternal life" (25:46). In his own words, Jesus has made it clear that his message has to do above all with the kingdom of heaven. His teaching may be summarized in one key idea: righteousness, which is considered the ticket, task, and goal of God's kingdom.

But Jesus was not the first teacher to talk about righteousness or justice—*ṣdaqah* in Hebrew. In fact, this term is used over five hundred times in the Hebrew scriptures, and usually in one of three ways. It can refer to a divine trait ("You are righteous, O LORD, and your judgments are right," Ps. 119:137), right relationship ("You are more righteous than I; for you have repaid me good, whereas I have repaid you evil," 1 Sam. 24:17) and right conduct ("Justice, and only justice, you shall pursue, so that you may live and occupy the land that the Lord your God is giving you," Deut. 16:20). Like God the Father, Jesus the Son is righteous in his personal character. He acts in right relationship with God when he is baptized by John, even though John declines to do it at first, and he commands his followers to behave rightly in accordance with the intention of the law and the prophets. For this reason New Testament scholar Leander Keck calls Matthew's Jesus the "righteous teacher of righteousness."

In Matthew's gospel, Jesus delivers five major discourses:

- The Sermon on the Mount (chapters 5–7),
- the mission to the Jews (chapter 10),
- the mystery of the kingdom of heaven (chapter 13),
- the preservation of church order (chapter 18), and
- the preparation for the final judgment (chapters 24–25).

These discourses represent Jesus' major thinking on the kingdom of heaven and contain sample teachings that showcase his wisdom as a religious teacher. They are the specialized knowledge by which Jesus stunned the religious elites and won his reputation as a teacher of God's will. Reading these five discourses as a compendium of Jesus' ideas, we may ask what they reveal about Jesus' theological conviction, worldview, and moral vision. We may also learn how he defines righteousness for the kingdom of heaven and how he advises his followers to face the final reckoning with God. Many of his ideas have become basic principles of Christian ethics and social standards in Western civilization. Their impact on the life of believers, the mission of the church, and the ethos of the society is deep and evident, even when scholars debate about their contemporary applications.

In this chapter, we do not have space to discuss the whole of Jesus' teaching, so we will examine only a few sayings that are influential or controversial to gain a glimpse into Jesus' view of the kingdom of heaven and righteousness. Our purpose is to see what Jesus might have meant to say and then how Matthew and later interpreters appropriated them for their own day. With a brief critical reflection on different interpretations, it is our hope to find some proper ways to apply Jesus' challenging teachings to our life today.

The Sermon on the Mount

The Sermon on the Mount is a major collection of Jesus' sayings on the needed attitudes and conduct for the kingdom of heaven. Scholar Hans Dieter Betz calls this discourse an "epitome"; it contains Jesus' principal ideas for his disciples to internalize and reflect upon. Strictly speaking, these are not laws to be kept literally, but principles to guide their lives in a new context. This sermon is full of Jesus' insights on divine character, human nature, and moral vision; it has been called the Magna Carta of the kingdom of heaven.

BLESSED ARE THE POOR IN SPIRIT (5:3–12)

Jesus begins his sermon with the beatitudes, announcing divine blessings for those who are in need and those who are virtuous. In literary form, beatitude is a saying in two parts. The first part ("Blessed are the poor in spirit") describes a human character or behavior that is to be blessed, while the second part ("for theirs is the kingdom of heaven") promises a divine reward now or in the future.

This genre is often used in wisdom literature, and one well-known example can be found in the psalms:

> Happy are those who do not follow the advice of the wicked, or take the path that sinners tread, or sit in the seat of scoffers; but their delight is in the law of the LORD, and on his law they meditate day and night. They are like trees planted by streams of water, which yield their fruit in its season, and their leaves do not wither. In all that they do, they prosper. (Ps. 1:1–3)

Using the form of beatitude to teach, Jewish sages often emphasize the first part ("Blessed") for the purpose of moral exhortation. They urge young people to think rightly and behave properly in order to harvest success and happiness in life.

Beatitudes are also found in apocalyptic literature in the Second Temple period, such as the words spoken to the martyrs in 1 Enoch: "Blessed are you, righteous and elect ones, for glorious is your portion" (1 Enoch 58:2). In contrast to the sages, these visionaries tend to emphasize the apodosis and highlight the divine rewards as God's grace. Their purpose is to reassure their readers of God's unfailing care so as to infuse them with hope while enduring suffering for the sake of faith.

In light of his apocalyptic message—"the kingdom of heaven has come near" (3:2)—Jesus' beatitudes are most probably meant to reassure his followers of God's favor. Divine rewards are given both to the virtuous and the needy. God's promises rather than human merit are Jesus' main concern, so his beatitudes are words of comfort. Matthew certainly believes that in Jesus the new age of God's grace has begun. However, when he puts Jesus' beatitudes together in the Sermon on the Mount, which is intended to be acted on as new laws, he has transformed them into ethical teachings and presented them as rules of exhortation. He hopes to cultivate new character and new behaviors in his readers in the same way the Jewish sages did. This fits Matthew's purpose to turn his readers into disciples of Jesus.

> In light of his apocalyptic message—"the kingdom of heaven has come near" (3:2)—Jesus' beatitudes are most probably meant to reassure his followers of God's favor.

Because both the apocalyptic and wisdom readings are possible, the beatitudes have been interpreted either as divine comfort or spiritual discipline in the history of the church. In the first few centuries, most interpreters follow Matthew's didactic interpretation to read them as a list of virtues that believers should live into. In the fourth century, theologian John Chrysostom called the beatitudes "the foundations of His new polity" to which believers should pay strict attention. The beatitudes are new laws for all Christians to obey, and the "poor in spirit" in the first beatitude means not only humility but also contriteness, because confession of sins is the first step to reconciliation with God and the new life.

In one of his sermons Augustine of Hippo proposed an ingenious reading that turned out to be consequential in shaping later interpretations. To begin with, he considered the ninth beatitude ("Blessed are you . . . on my account," 5:11) an application of the eighth on persecution ("Blessed are those . . . for righteousness' sake," 5:10). Augustine further pointed out that the first and the eighth beatitude repeat one another, because both have the same reward ("for theirs is the kingdom of heaven"). In essence, he argued, there are seven beatitudes, and these seven beatitudes are the seven spiritual steps leading the human soul to ascend from repentance to perfection. On this spiritual journey, the soul begins with humility, which leads to the realization of its sinfulness and a deep grief over the loss of the highest good. At the fourth step, the soul hungers and thirsts for righteousness, by which it grows to be merciful in character and becomes pure in heart. At the seventh step, it finally acquires wisdom, "bringing peace to the whole man and effecting a likeness to God." Moreover, Augustine compares the seven beatitudes to the seven gifts of the Spirit in the prophecy of Isaiah, which are parallel steps in reverse:

> A shoot shall come out from the stump of Jesse, and a branch shall grow out of his roots. The spirit of the LORD shall rest on him, the spirit of wisdom and understanding, the spirit of counsel and might, the spirit of knowledge and the fear of the LORD. (Isa. 11:1–2)

If the soul begins its spiritual journey with the fear of God, it will then acquire the knowledge of God, rely on God's might, and follow God's counsel. Then it will obtain the understanding of God's will and gain the wisdom of God's plan to finally enjoy eternal rest in God. Since the passage from Isaiah is considered a messianic scripture in Christian tradition, it is not accidental that Augustine finds it closely related to Christian life.

Augustine's interpretation made a profound impact on the spiritual formation in the Catholic tradition. In the twelfth century, Hugh of St. Victor, for instance, followed this approach to find two more patterns of seven for comparison. Hugh concluded that the seven petitions of the Lord's Prayer reinforce the seven beatitudes and the seven gifts of the Spirit to provide a seven-step spiritual discipline that may guide human souls to reach perfection before God. These seven steps then serve as biblical prescriptions for the cure of the seven cardinal sins (wrath, greed, sloth, pride, lust, envy, and gluttony) that corrupt human souls.

A former Augustinian monk, Martin Luther was also influenced by Augustine's view of the beatitudes as parallels to the seven gifts of the Spirit. As a reformer, however, he was convinced that God's grace is necessary for both redemption and spiritual life. While claiming the beatitudes as grace, Luther recognized that they were also commandments to be merciful, humble, and "poor in spirit." The beatitudes are at the same time good news of God's grace, on the one hand, and new laws to be obeyed on the other. Because Christians live in two kingdoms (the sacred and the secular), however, Luther insisted that civil laws should be followed in secular world so that peace and order could be maintained.

Reading the beatitudes as steps to perfection reminds us to live our new life with spiritual discipline so that we may be transformed to serve as the salt of the earth and the light of the world.

To many Christians, the beatitudes are among the most beloved scriptures. How do we understand them? Learning from Jesus, Matthew, and other interpreters, I think we can regard them as both words of divine grace and rules of spiritual discipline. Reading the beatitudes as God's free gifts encourage us to embrace by faith God's blessings made available in Christ. Reading them as steps to perfection reminds us to live our new life with spiritual discipline so that we may be transformed to serve as the salt of the earth and the light of the world.

DO NOT RETALIATE, LOVE YOUR ENEMIES (5:38–48)

After preaching the beatitudes, Jesus declares that he has come not to abolish but to fulfill the law and the prophets. Anyone who wishes to enter the kingdom of heaven should exhibit a life of righteousness greater than that of the Pharisees. To help his disciples understand what he means by righteousness, Jesus uses six antithetical statements to demand the higher standard that God intended in the law, but that the human community has eroded. These new commandments govern human minds (anger and lust), interpersonal relationships (marriage and oath), and community life (evildoer and enemies). To avoid murder, Jesus commands his followers not to get angry, and to prevent adultery, he asks them to restrain from lustful thoughts. To protect marriage, he urges them to shun infidelity; to be credible, they must avoid swearing an oath; to end the cycle of violence, they must give up revenge. Finally, to overcome evil with goodness, he encourages them to love their enemies. In these commandments, Jesus sets the bar very high for human mind, relationship, and community. Some might think that Jesus is building a fence around the law, as the rabbis did in issuing *halakhah*—a set of rules and practices governing every aspect of Jewish life. If people strive to obey Jesus' stricter commandments, they may be protected from violating the law even if they have failed in the first instance. However, since he emphasizes that breaking his commandments will incur divine punishment, Jesus is really announcing the higher demands of the kingdom of heaven, which fulfill the law and the prophets as God originally intended.

Many people will agree that the most challenging commandments of all are the final two: resist no evildoers and love your enemies (5:39, 44). The Jewish law of *lex talionis*—"an eye for an eye and a tooth for a tooth"—is a just law, upholding the principle of proportionality to deter future crime, avoid excessive revenge, and prevent blood feuds. But why does Jesus also require victims to forfeit their legal right to seek reasonable compensations from their persecutors? It is not fair. In fact, Jesus asks them to go one step further, to turn the other cheek, give up their cloak, walk the second mile, and give to anyone who asks. Why does Jesus condone the perpetrators of crime and risk encouraging aggression? This commandment is indeed counterintuitive, but it indicates Jesus' conviction that his disciples should overcome evil with goodness. Violence engenders more violence, so he urges his disciples to leave vengeance to God who is just, especially now that the kingdom of heaven has come near.

Noble as it sounds, Jesus' commandment to love our enemies raises further questions. It is natural for people to love those who love them and hate those who hurt them, so why should Jesus' disciples love their enemies and pray for their persecutors? Again, it is not fair. Jesus seems keenly aware of the question, however, and he offers a theological reason to explain why he has given this commandment that runs so counter to human nature. As children of God, he argues, his disciples should imitate their heavenly Father, who "makes his sun rise on the evil and on the good, and sends rain on the righteous and on the unrighteous" (5:45). Like father, like son. Because their heavenly Father is perfect in love, they should also be perfect in love. To hate enemies is human; to forgive is divine. Only when believers develop the character of divine virtue can they garner the necessary spiritual strength to love the unlovable and pray for their oppressors. It is by such an unusual act of love that Jesus' disciples are distinguished from others. It is only by such extraordinary love, rather than by eloquent debate or exercise of power, that Matthew's besieged church could fend off the attacks of the rabbis and the synagogue.

These two sayings are very difficult indeed to put into practice. Nonetheless the early Christians followed them literally, enduring persecutions and martyrdom with remarkable resilience; consequently their witness and endurance conquered even the bloodiest Roman persecutors. Eventually, however, interpreters tended to blunt the radical demand of these two sayings after Christians began to hold high positions of political authority and social responsibility under the emperor Constantine. Augustine in particular felt compelled to develop a "just war" theory, which allowed the use of force to defend the innocent against their enemies when it was necessary, proportional, and the last resort.

During the Reformation, moreover, after witnessing the widespread destruction caused by the anarchy of the Peasants War, Martin Luther also gave Christian princes permission to use force in order to uphold law and order. It was he who developed the doctrine of "the two kingdoms," whereby the earthly kingdom is ruled by human laws, which included the use of military force, and the heavenly kingdom by divine grace. The Sermon on the Mount thus applies only to religious life and church community. When Christians began to exercise power in their society, they tended to pay closer attention to the different contexts to which the two sayings of Jesus are to be applied, and thereby to domesticate Jesus' radical teaching regarding nonviolence and reconciliation. From time to time, however, the world is stunned by the transforming power of Jesus' teaching when they see, for instance, how figures like Mahatma Gandhi and Martin Luther King adopted the principle of nonviolence resistance to liberate India from the British Empire and to earn civil rights for the African Americans in the United States. The reception history of the Sermon on the Mount shows that Jesus' radical teaching on resisting no evildoers and loving one's enemies, when willingly and faithfully practiced, are life-changing not only for personal spiritual formation and church mission, but also for political struggles and social reforms.

THE LORD'S PRAYER (6:9–13)

In his teaching on the practice of piety—that is, almsgiving, prayer, and fasting—Jesus emphasizes the importance of sincerity. It is significant to note that the Greek word for "piety" is "righteousness" (6:1), which suggests that all pious acts should be conducted in the right relationship with God. Jesus reminds us that before God all hearts are open and no secret is hidden. The all-knowing God watches everyone's inner thoughts as well as external behaviors, and will reward them justly. While practicing piety, we should avoid vainglory and hypocrisy.

Most noteworthy is the Lord's Prayer, which teaches the disciples what to pray and how to pray. It reflects Jesus' main concerns about the kingdom of heaven, which is why New Testament scholar Joachim Jeremias finds in it an outline of Jesus' theology. Most important is the address to God as "our Father" who is "in heaven." To call God "Father" is a familiar idea for Christians today, but it was a revolutionary idea in Jesus' time. After the exile in Babylon, the Jews realized how badly they had broken the covenant with God and, in the spirit of repentance, they paid special honor to God as the one and only holy Creator and acknowledged their own sinfulness. For the religious

The Lord's Prayer reflects Jesus' main concerns about the kingdom of heaven, and in it we find an outline of Jesus' theology.

establishment of Jesus' day, it was considered far too presumptuous to call the holy God one's "Father," so Jesus was condemned for blasphemy by the high priest Caiaphas the moment that he admitted that he was the Son of God (26:65).

By teaching his disciples to call on God as their father in prayer, Jesus grants them a new identity as God's children. In contrast to the version in Luke 11:2, Matthew adds "our" to make it a corporate prayer and thus remind us that we are all brothers and sisters to one another. Prayer is thus a family talk, and because of that we can confide everything to God, knowing that God will listen to us with interest. Matthew also adds "who are in heaven" to reassure us. Because God is taking charge from above, there is nothing in the world which is too difficult for God to solve.

The first three petitions of the Lord's Prayer teach us to mind God's business first—God's honor, God's kingdom, and God's will. Very often we pray to God when we are in need, as if God were a kind of mail-order service. If we regard prayer as a family talk, however, we should think of God our Father's desires as more important than our own wishes. Giving priority to God's desires can set our relationship right with God ("hallowed be thy name"), our perspective right with the world ("thy kingdom come"), and our wishes right for ourselves ("thy will be done"). It shows that we are committing ourselves to the service of God our Father as Lord.

Jesus also teaches us to ask God boldly to meet our needs: daily bread, divine forgiveness, avoidance of temptation, and protection from evil. Jesus knows that we have legitimate needs in body, in mind, in spirit, and in soul. Because God is our Father, we can count on his daily provision and timely protection to enjoy life, peace, freedom, and safety. Because the almighty and gracious God will be happy to answer our prayers, there is no surprise that in many ancient manuscripts this prayer ends with an added doxology: "For the kingdom and the power and the glory are yours forever."

SAVE NO MONEY AND TRUST IN YOUR FATHER IN HEAVEN (6:19–34)

Living in the pain and anxiety of economic recession and financial crisis, we have seen many jobs lost, houses repossessed, businesses bankrupted, pensions vaporized, lives destroyed, and dreams smashed. Under the circumstances, how can Jesus command, "Do not store up for yourselves treasures on earth" but put your trust instead in treasures in heaven? How does this make any sense? Doesn't the Old Testament teach that wealth is a blessing from God? Don't we need financial resources to help the poor? Living in a capitalist society, we know very well that money talks, so how might we understand Jesus' point? Fortunately, Jesus explains what he means to say. First, heavenly treasures are more valuable, because earthly treasures do not last long. Second, loving God is more important than piling up wealth, because no one can serve wealth without becoming its slave. Third, there is no need to worry about how we are to live because God will take care of our necessities. Therefore, Jesus tells us, "Strive first for the kingdom of God and his righteousness, and all these things will be given to you as well" (6:33).

By pointing out the limited worth but irresistible seduction of wealth, Jesus urges his disciples to trust and serve God, the source of all blessings, as the most valuable pursuit in life. God's kingdom and righteousness ought to be the priority. Matthew knew that many of his readers were suffering under heavy taxation and economic exploitation under the Roman Empire, so that the pursuit of money had to be their primary concern, so he recorded these sayings of Jesus to reassure them of God's loving care and encourage them to trust in God without worry.

Jesus' view of money is countercultural. Most people understand that money cannot buy all happiness, but know that poverty will not bring much joy either. Greed for money is the root of evil, but to be free of worry can lead to idleness too. Thus one main issue in the history of interpreting the scriptures has always been—is it possible to make money and love God at the same time? Before the time of Matthew's gospel, Paul was already concerned that some Christians in Thessalonica and Rome might take Jesus' saying at its plain sense and become busybodies or idlers, so he advised Christians to work hard and earn money so that they may help the poor: "And we urge you, beloved, to admonish the idlers, encourage the faint hearted, help the weak, be patient with all of them" (1 Thess. 5:14; Rom. 12:11).

In a famous sermon called "What Kind of Rich Man Can Enter the Kingdom of God?" second-century theologian Clement of Alexandria tried to answer the question by dividing the rich into different categories. Those who are not enslaved by wealth and are willing to use their wealth for charity, he argued, are not the rich whom Jesus condemns, but will be able to enter the kingdom of God. Even though priests, monks, and nuns did follow Jesus' teaching to take the vow of poverty, most interpreters did not think making money is wrong in itself as long as the wealth is used for almsgiving or the mission of the church. In the eighteenth century, when so many poor people suffered in the slums of London while rich factory owners enjoyed the enormous wealth gathered from England's new industries, John Wesley was concerned about Christian view of money as well. His three points—"Gain all you can, save all you can, and give all you can"—eloquently argued in the sermon "On the Use of Money," have been well accepted by many faithful Christians as prudent principles as they try to strike a balance between serving God and accruing wealth.

One major debate on how to interpret the Sermon on the Mount is whether Jesus' teaching can be practiced in real life. There are two competing views. Thomas Aquinas conceded that Jesus' sayings in that discourse are so demanding that nobody can fulfill them, so he proposed a "two-standard" theory. He divided those sayings into two kinds: "commandments," which are necessary laws required of all believers who wish to be saved, and "gospel counsels," which are optional directions provided for religious people seeking perfection. Laws that are more demanding, such as resisting no evil doers and saving no money, are thus reserved for the religious elites such as priests, monks, and nuns, while the laity are held to a lesser standard. During the Reformation Martin Luther also recognized that nobody could fully obey the laws of Christ as set out in the Sermon on the Mount because they function not as "rule" but as "mirror," reflecting back to people their sin and deficiency before the high standard of God's will. In a sermon Luther wrote:

> We cannot be justified or saved through the teaching of the Law, which only brings us to the knowledge of ourselves, the knowledge that by our own ability we cannot properly fulfill an iota of it. . . . We can never take our stand before God on this basis, but we must always creep to Christ.*

---

*Martin Luther, The Sermon on the Mount (Sermons) and the Magnificat in Luther's Works, Vol. 21; ed. tr. Jaroslav Pelikan (St. Louis, MO: Concordia, 1956), 72.

It is true that Jesus' teaching sets such a high standard for human hearts and human behavior that even the most dedicated believers find it extremely difficult to follow. But it is also true that Jesus wanted all his followers, not only the few pious, to be perfect as their heavenly Father is perfect. It is by doing Jesus' words, not simply calling him Lord, that they enter the kingdom of heaven. The disciples will be wise to learn to obey his commandments, so that they may build their spiritual houses on the rock, which may withstand the severest storms, than upon sand.

> *Martin Luther recognized that nobody could fully obey the laws of Christ as set out in the Sermon on the Mount because they function not as "rule" but as "mirror," reflecting back to people their sin and deficiency.*

Mission and Inclusivity

In Matthew 10, Jesus sends out the twelve disciples on a mission with these instructions, "Go nowhere among the Gentiles, and enter no town of the Samaritans, but go rather to the lost sheep of the house of Israel" (10:5–6). To us this idea may be disturbing. Why does Jesus seem prejudiced against the Gentiles and the Samaritans? Is not God impartial, as Peter said after baptizing Cornelius the centurion in Caesarea? How would Matthew's ethnically mixed church respond to a mission intended explicitly for the Jews? Most important of all, how do we understand inclusivity in the church and mission to the world today?

To answer these questions, we need to consider Matthew's point of view on history. To begin with, it is safe to assume that the author of this gospel was aware of the discriminatory tone of this hard saying. After all, in Antioch Peter and Paul had a public brawl over the table fellowship between the Jewish and Gentile Christians, as attested in Paul's letter to the Galatians. According to Acts 15, Peter, James, and Paul also met in Jerusalem to debate and decide how Gentile Christians could become members of the church without discrimination. Thus by Matthew's time, the ethnic issue had been resolved at least in theory. To include this hard saying in his gospel, Matthew must have a theological reason beyond preserving it as a historical record. To find that reason, it is important to remember that he has included another saying on mission at the end of his gospel, in the form of the Great Commission: "Go therefore and make disciples of all nations" (28:19). It is clear, then, that Matthew did not oppose the mission to the Gentiles, for in his gospel Jesus dispatched two missions at two different points in time: the first to the Jews when he was in Galilee, and the second to all nations after his resurrection. Considered side by side, these two missions reflect Matthew's perspective on God's work in time: God has a salvation plan for all humanity, but it is carried out in temporal sequence, first to the Jews and then the Gentiles. The same idea, which theologians call "salvation history," can be found in Paul, who declared in his letter to the Romans: "For I am not ashamed of the gospel; it is the power of God for salvation to everyone who has faith, to the Jew first and also to the Greek" (Rom 1:16).

The goal of the first mission was to tell the Jews that God had sent the promised Messiah, and Jesus' healing miracles proved that the kingdom of heaven had drawn near. After being raised from the dead, Jesus sent his disciples on a second mission to teach the whole world about God's love, so that all peoples may belong to God through baptism and become Jesus' disciples by learning to obey his commandments. For everything there is a time and season. The prohibition against the Gentiles and the Samaritans in chapter 10, therefore, is time specific and it only applies to the first mission. Historians have also suggested that perhaps the two missions reflect two separate efforts in the early church to bring the gospel first to the Jews and then to the Gentiles, for which Peter is called "the apostle to the Jews" and Paul "the apostle to the Gentiles." In Matthew's view, both missions are valid and important, for all are God's children. Theologically, the first mission demonstrates God's covenant faithfulness to his chosen people while the second is a sign of God's inclusive love to all nations. Together they declare Jesus as the savior of both the Jews and the Gentiles.

When we read the accounts of these two missions together, we can also better understand the disturbing story of the Canaanite woman who pleads with Jesus to heal her daughter, who is tormented by demons. This story is upsetting to a modern audience because Jesus seems so reluctant to help her, citing as his reason, "I was sent only to the lost sheep of the house of Israel" (15:24). Jesus even uses a racial slur: "It is not fair to take the children's food and throw it to the dogs" (15:26). But this Gentile mother loves her daughter and, insisting on God's love, humbly and firmly replies, "Yes, Lord, yet even the dogs eat the crumbs that fall from their masters' table" (v. 27). Such unbending love and such gentle power from a caring mother finally changes Jesus' mind about his exclusive mission to the Jews. As a result, he praises her faith and grants her wish, healing her daughter instantly. It seems that Jesus understands his mission as first and foremost to the Jews, but he is willing to change his position and show the disciples how God also loves the Gentiles. This woman becomes a precursor of God's love for the Gentiles and a model of faith. As a resurrection people, therefore, we should be open to the new things that the Spirit of God may do and be willing to welcome all peoples into the church to share God's grace.

The second disturbing question in Matthew's mission discourse of chapter 10 is this: why does Jesus order his disciples to travel light? He warns them about the danger on the road and the risk of hostile persecution; nonetheless he advises them, "Take no gold, or silver, or copper in your belts, no bag for your journey, or two tunics, or sandals, or a staff; for laborers deserve their food" (10:9–10). What is Jesus' meaning? Because missionaries are God's laborers, God will provide for them through the generosity of the people who accept their good news about the kingdom of heaven. It shows that Jesus is confident that they will win converts and that God's protection is reliable. This optimistic view of mission has inspired many missionary efforts in history and brought the gospel to all corners of the world, but his instruction is not always easy to follow. Missionaries, whether domestic or cross-cultural, and mission works of varied kinds, will often encounter hardship, resistance, and even persecution. But "have no fear of them," Jesus says, because God will protect us (10:26). Jesus' teaching on mission continues to summon us to bring the gospel in words and deeds to the lost people of God, and as we do, we can trust in God' provision and protection without fear.

Parables of the Kingdom of Heaven

From a boat in the sea of Galilee, Jesus tells seven parables to the crowds on the beach, parables that illustrate the extraordinary nature, power, and value of the kingdom of heaven. Two of these parables are particularly noteworthy because Jesus also provides an interpretation of their meaning. The first concerns a sower who spreads his seeds indiscriminately—on the path, on rocky ground, and among thorns, as well as in good soil. Jesus likens the sower to himself, suggesting that he is impartial in spreading the word of God. The same gospel is preached to all; it is everyone's to lose or to gain. The parable also tells us that the quality of the soil does matter—"the one who hears the word and understands it" (13:23)—because in the end it is only in fertile ground that the seeds grow into plants and bear plentiful fruit. Besides emphasizing the good news of God's grace for all, Jesus' parable of the sower is also an exhortation to accept his life-transforming message so that we may grow spiritually and testify to the bounteous blessings of God.

> *Jesus likens the sower to himself, suggesting that he is impartial in spreading the word of God. The same gospel is preached to all; it is everyone's to lose or to gain.*

The second parable of the kingdom is that of the weeds among the wheat. A man sows a field of wheat, but an "enemy" comes at night and plants weeds among the good crop, so they grow together in the field. When the servants come and ask their master whether they should uproot the weeds, they are told

> No, for in gathering the weeds you would uproot the wheat along with them. Let both of them grow together until the harvest; and at harvest time I will tell the reapers, "Collect the weeds first and bind them in bundles to be burned, but gather the wheat into my barn." (13:29–30)

Thus, even though the farmer knows that the weeds have been planted by his enemies, he advises his servants to be patient and leave the final judgment to God. Depending on how we understand the symbol of the field, this parable explains why there are good and bad people in the church and in the world, and encourages us to take no judgment into our own hands but leave it to the all-knowing God who will separate the righteous from the wicked in the final judgment. God loves all people and hates to see anyone perish, so we need to examine ourselves, making sure that we are the wheat, not the weeds. God will render justice at the end. Even as wicked people seem to prosper in the world, God is not tardy but wants to give people a second chance. If God loves to forgive rather than to punish, how much more so should we the children of God treat one another in the church and in the world?

Community Life

While traveling through Capernaum, the disciples ask Jesus, "Who is the greatest in the kingdom of heaven?" Jesus calls a child to stand among them and replies, "Truly I tell you, unless you change and become like children, you will never enter the kingdom of heaven. Whoever becomes humble like this child is the greatest in the kingdom of heaven" (18:1–4).

With this answer Jesus turns their expectations—and ours—upside down. We expect our leaders to be mature and confident, but here Jesus defines them as people who are like children, vulnerable and humble. The first quality of church leadership is thus humility. Only those who honor God and respect others as much as they do themselves can serve as leaders of the church. Here Jesus takes the opportunity to teach his two important responsibilities of leadership in the church. First of all, leaders should be mindful of their community, especially the "little ones who believe in me" under their care, that is, members who are economically poor, socially despised, or spiritually weak. They should lead by personal example and be very careful not to become a stumbling block to their most vulnerable members. For if they should cause anyone to fail in faith, Jesus says, "It would be better for you if a great millstone were fastened around your neck and you were drowned in the depth of the sea" (18:6). Jesus also admonishes leaders not to despise or ignore the weak and vulnerable because "their angels continually see the face of my Father in heaven" (18:10).

In the second place, leaders should promote reconciliation at all cost. Even though personal conflict is inevitable in any community, Jesus wants us to persuade anyone who is guilty of wrongdoing to repent—first by talking to him privately and then with a committee of witnesses, before the case is finally decided by the whole community for discipline. Jesus also tells Peter that he should forgive one who sins against him "not seven times, but, I tell you, seventy-seven times" (18:22). The parable that follows is about a servant who, although he is forgiven a huge debt by his master, in turn refuses to forgive his fellow servant for a little debt and is punished for his hardness of heart:

> And in anger his lord handed him over to be tortured until he should pay his entire debt. So my heavenly Father will also do to every one of you, if you do not forgive your brother or sister from your heart. (18:34–35)

In this discourse, Jesus highlights the care for the vulnerable and the willingness to forgive others as two of the most important tasks for church leadership, which still remains true for any healthy community today.

Parables of the Last Judgment

Finally, in Jerusalem, Jesus delivers his fifth discourse, which urges his disciples to be vigilant about the final judgment. In four parables, three repeated warnings deserve attention. First, Jesus tells his followers that the coming of the Son of Man at the end of time will be "delayed" (24:48; 25:5), but it will surely come. He will come on the clouds with power and glory, and will send out his angels to gather all people in the world for judgment—"but about that day and hour no one knows, neither the angels of heaven, nor the Son, but only the Father" (24:36). Clearly, then, no one should speculate on the time of the final judgment. Throughout history there have been countless self-proclaimed prophets who claim to have revealed knowledge about the date of the end of the world and caused much anxiety and disillusion among their followers. There are also people who deny the whole concept of the final judgment as mere mythology, but it is to those who dismiss the final judgment that Jesus tells his parables of warning:

> Keep awake therefore, for you do not know on what day your Lord is coming. But understand this: if the owner of the house had known in what part of the night the thief was coming, he would have stayed awake and would not have let his house be broken into. Therefore you also must be ready, for the Son of Man is coming at an unexpected hour. (24:42–44)

Because the return of the master and the bridegroom is delayed, servants will neglect their duties and bridesmaids will not prepare extra oil for their lamps. The servant who buries his talents underground finds excuses by blaming it on the harshness of his master, but God's judgment will be fair and final. The servants who are good and worthy will be given eternal life; those who are wicked and lazy will be sent to eternal punishment. The bridesmaids who have sufficient oil for their lamps will go into the wedding feast, but the rest will be left behind. Matthew's message is clear: "Keep awake, therefore, for you do not know on what day your Lord is coming."

These parables also teach that we will all be judged by our actions. Membership or leadership in the church cannot guarantee survival; only those who have borne the fruits of righteousness will be able to enter the kingdom of heaven. Matthew's church may have fallen into spiritual complacency, taking God's grace for granted and risking their eternal life. It is to show the consequences of this complacency that Matthew adds his own distinctive ending to the parable of the wedding banquet. Even though he has been freely invited, the guest wearing no wedding robe is thrown out when the king arrives, cast into "outer darkness," for many are called but few are chosen (22:11–14). Doing righteousness is therefore a deadly serious matter. As in the parable of the sheep and the goats, only those who feed the hungry, quench the thirsty, clothe the naked, care for the sick, and visit the imprisoned are called righteous and ushered into the eternal kingdom (25:37–40).

> Matthew's church may have fallen into spiritual complacency, taking God's grace for granted, and to warn of the consequences Matthew adds his own distinctive ending to the parable of the wedding banquet.

Matthew's third point is that the final judgment is universal, but it will begin with the faith community and its leaders. All people in the world will stand before the king and be separated into two groups, either righteous or wicked. It is noteworthy that the main characters in these parables are servants in charge of the household, bridesmaids who serve the bride, and servants who are given the master's wealth to manage. These are no ordinary members, but leaders and teachers of the church, and they will have to give an account of themselves before God. Leaders and teachers have been granted special tasks, privileges, and gifts; it is their duty to teach all believers to obey Jesus' commandments and become disciples. Accordingly, they must take special heed of the fact that leadership is responsibility.

In our time many people do not believe in the final judgment or the end of the world. Over against the popular stories in the "Left Behind" series, the final judgment is thought to be mythological language expressing an ancient worldview; it symbolizes the ultimate justice. In a scientific age, we fear that the world may come to an end because of environmental disaster or nuclear explosion, but not because of the return of Christ. Other people, including Christians, object to the idea of the final judgment because they believe in a loving God who could not bear to destroy his own creation, even unrepentant sinners. Sinners will suffer from their own miseries in life, but not from eternal punishment. Obviously our view of the world and our theological convictions will determine how we understand the final judgment and how to respond to Jesus' warnings about it. In a way, the question of the final judgment is similar to that of the resurrection—the Bible testifies to their historical factuality and insists on their theological importance. One aspect of this question deserves our careful consideration. If there is no resurrection, then Jesus' crucifixion meant that he was merely a political victim and not a savior. By the same token, if there is no final judgment, Jesus' warnings and cautionary parables meant that he was merely a religious charlatan, and not a revealer of truth. If the final judgment is only a threat to coerce believers into a way of life based on righteousness, there will be no real justice, and God does not have the final word. At the very least, Jesus' warning about the final judgment challenges us to reflect seriously about the quality and the accountability of our lives.

> *Our view of the world and our theological convictions will determine how we understand the final judgment and how to respond to Jesus' warnings about it.*

A Teacher of God's Will

The remarkable teachings in these five discourses reveal Jesus' wisdom as a teacher of God's will, setting forth his convictions about righteousness, God's mission, the kingdom of heaven, the community of believers, and the final judgment. What can we learn from Jesus' teaching that applies to our own lives?

First, God is our Father. Beneath Jesus' teaching lies the fundamental conviction that God is our Father in heaven. The almighty God who created the world knows, loves, and cares for us. God is both transcendent and immanent, both hidden and approachable; we can always count on God's provision and protection, and enjoy communion with God. Because God is our Father, we become brothers and sisters and the church is a family. This radical view of God gives us a new identity and new relationship.

Second, we are offered a new way of being. As children of God and siblings to one another, we are a new people, sharing the same character that God has exhibited through Christ. Like our heavenly Father who is perfect in love, it is our duty to love even our enemies as well as one another. In a world where so many people suffer from broken relationships—in the family, in the church, in the society, and among nations—living into the new way of being means to be always willing to forgive those who offend us and love those who hate us, so that enmity may be eradicated and reconciliation be made.

Third, we are invited into a new way of life. The kingdom of heaven demands that the people of God enter a new way of life. Merely listening to Jesus' teaching is not sufficient; only those who act on his words will be like the wise man in the parable who builds his house on rock, which no rain, flood, or wind can damage (7:24–7). In other words, we need to become Jesus' disciples, learning to obey all that he has commanded. It is not easy, because his teachings often challenge us at the level of our basic instincts, which are self-centered and self-interested. His radical teachings, however, are given precisely to help us live up to the new vision of the kingdom of heaven and the high calling of God's righteousness. If we strive first to obey them, God will help.

> *Merely listening to Jesus' teaching is not sufficient; only those who act on his words will be like the wise man in the parable who builds his house on rock, which no rain, flood, or wind can damage (7:24–7).*

Fourth, we must believe not only in God's mercy, but also God's justice. Each of the five discourses is punctuated by a serious warning about the final judgment. Jesus wants his disciples to remember

God's grace but also be ready to answer to God's justice. It is not helpful to speculate on the schedule or details of the final judgment, but Jesus' earnest warnings about it summon us to live a transformed life with God at its center and our neighbor in its purview. God is the loving Father and the just judge at the same time. We should not turn God's generosity into cheap grace and expect no accountability.

Because Jesus' teaching is so idealistic, radical, and countercultural, one Jewish scholar, Joseph Klausner, calls it an "extremist morality" that "has not proved possible in practice." But is that estimate true? In recent years two events that took place in the United States caught the world's attention and shook our moral sense at its foundation. First is the terrorist attack of September 11, 2001. The hijackings and airstrikes at the World Trade Center and the Pentagon caused so many casualties and horrific destruction right in front of our eyes and hurt us so deeply in our souls that we cried out for revenge and swift justice. Our first instinct was to fight back. Heightened security against any suspicious person became the order of the day, and dismantling Al Qaeda our first priority. Under the circumstances, it would have seemed ridiculous and unpatriotic even to think about resisting no evildoers or loving our enemies.

Now that a decade has gone by, however, we may be able to begin to reflect on what has transpired in our antiterrorist war. We are thankful to the law enforcement for their hard work to ensure our security, and we appreciate the faith communities' efforts to foster dialogue among Christians and Muslims to avoid further clashes and hate crimes. At the same time, some important issues need to be raised. Has everything really changed so much that we can do anything we feel necessary in the name of national security? Is everything we do really good for us? What price have we paid, and what prospect do we have for the future? We went to war in Iraq and Afghanistan, losing thousands of our soldiers and countless number of their civilians—many times over the victims of the original attack, let alone the astronomical expenses of war and the total devastation of those two countries. We have also lost the presumed innocence and due process we used to enjoy in our society, but have we seriously considered the root causes of the hostility that was and still is directed against us? Can we find a way beyond revenge and wrath to end the hatred and pursue peace among all peoples? Despite the complex situation, it is not too naive to ask the question: is Jesus' teaching on loving enemies foolishly irrelevant, dangerously idealistic, or a high calling that may transform values and lives and promote new relationship? What would be the cost if we decided to follow it?

The second soul-shaking event is the remarkable Amish community at Nickel Mines, Pennsylvania, whose ten little girls were killed and injured in a senseless school shooting on October 2, 2006. That tragedy stunned the whole nation, but the Amish community astonished us even more not only with their readiness to forgive the gunman, but their request that we pray for the gunman's family. They showed us in the most unforgettable way how a virtuous Christian community can overcome an unbearable tragedy by following Jesus' radical commandments to take no revenge and love even our enemies. Such grace and such forgiveness remind us that there is an alternative way—the way of Christ—to end hostility among people. We are all children of God, who is perfect in love. In Paul's words, "God proves his love for us in that while we still were sinners Christ died for us." (Rom. 5:8). The Amish community has demonstrated that Jesus' sayings are radical, but not impossible to follow. As ethics scholar Stanley Hauerwas has argued, when a community of faith is thoroughly transformed by the love of God and follows Jesus' commandments to become a community of character, it can testify to the life-changing power of the kingdom of heaven with the virtues that are worthy of the children of God. Life is not easy and conflicts in relationship are often complex, so we should not take a simplistic approach toward interpersonal crisis. When we engage in a moral decision in life settings, we need to learn how to discern the priority (love or justice) and responsibility (personal or social) among the many thorny factors in each case, but Jesus' teachings—to overcome evil by goodness and to win over enemies with love—continue to summon us to pursue the perfect love that has been revealed in God's continuing care for the world and exemplified in Jesus' redemptive death on the cross. Love is the most excellent way that endures.

Precisely because Jesus' teaching seems so alien to our culture, we are forced to recognize the distance and the tension between Jesus' spiritual vision and that of ours. Counting the cost, do I want to follow Jesus as his disciple? I think many of us will feel trapped in a quandary. We want to say yes, because Jesus' vision of the kingdom of heaven is so uplifting and inspiring; we want to say no because his commandments are too demanding and inexpedient. It will be comforting to know, however, that Jesus understands that his way of righteousness is a narrow path. Discipleship is a pilgrimage, a journey of adventures through strange places that takes time and needs support before we can reach our destination. So Jesus encourages us: "But strive first for the kingdom of God and his righteousness, and all these things will be given to you as well" (6:33). Before we learn to become Jesus' disciples, we are already God's children. Our loving Father in heaven is glad to accompany us on this journey.

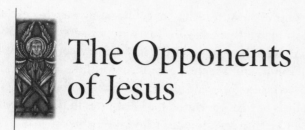

The Opponents of Jesus

Leaders often earn distinction by the caliber of their enemies. George Washington, for instance, is honored as a national hero because he led the newly constituted Continental Army to defeat the well-trained British Navy and won independence for the colonies. John F. Kennedy is remembered as a strong president because he stood firm against Nikita Khrushchev during the Cuban Missile Crisis and defused a possible nuclear war with the Soviet Union. Leadership is likewise often defined by the challenges one has to overcome. Archbishop Tutu, for example, earned the Nobel Peace Prize because he fearlessly preached against the apartheid system, legalized racial discrimination, to win equal rights for all peoples in South Africa. Mother Teresa of Calcutta received worldwide acclaim as a saint of mercy because she embraced and served the dying poor in India as Christ. Oftentimes, the tougher the enemies are, the more prominent these leaders become; the harsher their adversaries, the more inspiring their leadership can be. In Matthew's gospel, Jesus proves to be an eminent teacher of God's will partially by his words of wisdom and partially by outwitting his hostile opponents. His leadership is all the more distinguished because of the legal debates and political pressure he has to endure. Jesus is a wise teacher and a compassionate healer, so why do his opponents hate him so much and conspire to have him killed? How do their conflicts reveal Jesus' character traits and Matthew's concerns for the church?

From birth to death, Jesus encounters a number of hostile opponents. When he is born, King Herod the Great tries to trick the wise men from the East into revealing his whereabouts in order to have him killed. During his forty days in the wilderness, the devil tries to seduce him with tricky questions into seeking his own self-interest. As he becomes famous in Galilee, the Pharisees and the scribes accuse him of violating the law, hoping to discredit his teaching. While in Jerusalem, the chief priests and the elders, the Herodians and the Sadducees, join forces with the Pharisees to challenge his authority and entrap him. Even Pilate, the Roman governor, becomes an accomplice in Jesus' death. Finally, the Pharisees set up guards at Jesus' tomb to prevent his body from being stolen, suspecting his disciples would lie about his resurrection.

These conflict stories reveal not only his opponents' hypocrisy and wickedness but also Jesus' character and prowess as the Messiah, the Son of God, and the teacher of God's will. They also reflect the spiritual clash between the heavenly kingdom and the present world, and a cosmic war between God and the devil. As biblical scholar Jack Kingsbury has argued, the constant struggle between Jesus and his opponents also drives the development of the plot in Matthew's narrative. How Jesus, the mighty healer and the wise teacher, is rejected by the Jewish leaders thus becomes a focal point of Matthew's story. Their opposition and hostility explain why the Son of God ends up dying on the cross and yet the gospel of the kingdom of heaven is spread to all nations. What does Matthew want us to learn from these conflicts?

How Jesus, the mighty healer and the wise teacher, is rejected by the religious leadership thus becomes a focal point of Matthew's story.

King Herod

In Luke's gospel, Jesus' birth is a joyful event. The angels celebrate it with joyful carols in heaven and the shepherds in the field rush to visit the holy baby in the manger. This event is far gloomier in

Matthew—King Herod feels threatened by the news of the future king, so he slaughters a great number of babies in Bethlehem. The wise men must return to the East via another route, and the holy family becomes refugees in Egypt for a few years. This first conflict is resolved by divine intervention. Even though the political powers attempt to destroy baby Jesus, God protects him. King Herod's massacre of the infants demonstrates the brutality of the political power that seeks to dominate and control. But the divine intervention proves that God loves and saves Jesus as the beloved Son because God has a special plan for him—the infant is destined for a great future. The encounter between Jesus and Herod shows that no political power, even the one that has the authority to kill, can undermine God's life-giving grace.

The Devil

As a young man getting ready to start his ministry for the kingdom of heaven, Jesus is confronted by another opponent. The devil, the liar who successfully seduces Eve and Adam to disobey God in Genesis 2, tries to thwart God's plan of salvation by luring Jesus with three tricky questions. Jesus has been fasting in the desert for forty days and nights, so he is hungry, thirsty, and tired. The devil pretends to care about his physical well-being, suggesting that he turns stones into bread. This suggestion seems innocent enough, but Jesus is aware of the devil's scheme to challenge his status as the Son of God. If he does what the devil tells him to do, he may prove his divine status but will also inadvertently do the devil's bidding instead of God's. So Jesus quotes Scripture to refute the devil: "One does not live by bread alone, but by every word that comes from the mouth of the LORD" (Deut. 8:3). Spiritual food is more important than physical food, and listening to God is the only right thing to do.

Next, knowing that Jesus honors the word of God, the devil places him on the pinnacle of the temple in Jerusalem and cites a scriptural text (Ps. 91:11–12) to assure him that God's angels will protect him if he jumps off. Again, Jesus quotes Scripture to repudiate the devil: "Do not put the LORD your God to the test" (Deut. 6:16). God has indeed provided and protected the people of Israel on their journey in the desert, but they repeatedly test and irritate God with their disbelief. As an exemplary Son of God, Jesus shows us how one can trust God for help without testing God. Finally, the devil takes Jesus to a high mountain and promises to give him all the kingdoms of the world if he will only fall down and worship him. Hearing this proposal, Jesus rebukes the devil for the third time and sends it away, quoting again from Deuteronomy (6:13): "Worship the Lord your God, and serve only him" (Matt. 4:10). As the creator of the world and the Lord of history, only God deserves to be worshipped and adored. Anything else that tries to take priority over God is idol.

The three temptations that the devil offers Jesus in the desert can be found recurring throughout Jesus' ministry. From time to time, exhausted from healing a great number of people day and night, and frustrated by the rejection of such cities as Chorazin, Bethsaida, and Capernaum, Jesus needs to retreat to a foreign place, Tire and Sidon, for rest. Physical health is important to spiritual well-being. While in Jerusalem, Jesus is enraged when he finds the merchants defiling the temple, so he overturns their tables and seats and drives them out of the house of prayer without apology. No one should test God. Finally, after praying through the night in the garden of Gethsemane, Jesus submits himself to God's will by accepting the cross for the sake of sinners. He serves God alone.

The temptation story that begins Jesus' ministry, therefore, demonstrates how we can overcome any seduction—be it physical, spiritual, or political—that may divert God's children from obeying, trusting, and serving God alone. Our journey in life is part of the spiritual warfare between God and the devil. The devil often disguises itself as an innocent angel pretending to care about our needs, but aims at stirring up our desires for self-interest, pride, and ambition, distracting us from loving God with all our heart, soul, and mind. In his triumph over the devil, Jesus shows that the best way to overcome temptations is to follow the word of God in Scripture. Oftentimes, we think a little compromise may bring us to a win-win situation, but we can easily fall into spiritual danger when we bargain with the devil. Imitating Christ the obedient Son, however, we will be able to see the ugliness in the devil's beautiful lies and reject the idolatry of the world.

The Pharisees and the Scribes

In Matthew's gospel Jesus' most dogged opponents are the Pharisees, a group of pious Jews devoted to the learning and teaching of the law. Most of them are well educated and many serve as scribes. Occupying Moses' seat in the synagogues to teach the scriptures and explain the laws that govern religious and civil lives, the Pharisees assume a leadership role in the community. The scribes help people deal with official, commercial, and civil businesses, so they also command respect as social elites. Matthew paints a mixed picture of the Pharisees—some of them accept John the Baptist's baptism of repentance, though others are more interested in maintaining their own privileges and reputation. Jesus recognizes their righteousness (5:20) and commands his disciples to do what they teach though not what they do (23:2), but he also warns his disciples to beware of some of their teachings (16:6, 12). At the same time, however, these same Pharisees are a major source of opposition and hostility to Jesus' teachings, seeing him as a threat to the Temple authorities and conspiring to have him murdered.

> *Matthew paints a mixed picture of the Pharisees— some of them accept John the Baptist's baptism of repentance, though others are more interested in maintaining their own privileges and reputation.*

The Pharisees challenge Jesus for the first time when they find him sitting at dinner with tax collectors and sinners in Matthew's house. Tax collectors are despised because they work for the Romans to exploit the Jews and often overcharge taxes out of greed. Sinners are to be shunned for religious reasons. Because table fellowship is social embodiment of personal relationship, the Pharisees, who are concerned about the laws of purity, are appalled by Jesus' association with those people whom they consider deviant. By association, they figure that Jesus cannot be a holy person. However, the fact that Jesus changes Matthew the tax collector's life by calling him to be a disciple illustrates Jesus' point: "Those who are well have no need of a physician, but those who are sick. . . . For I have come to call not the righteous but sinners" (9:12–13). This conflict story reveals two opposite views of God: exclusive and inclusive. Jesus' mission is to save the lost sheep of the house of Israel, because the merciful God loves all children, especially those who need to be transformed.

The Pharisees also take great offense at Jesus' disciples because they pluck heads of grain to eat on the Sabbath, which entails working on a day of rest, and at Jesus because he heals a man with a withered hand on the same day. Jesus defends his hungry disciples by citing the incident in which David and his companions eat the bread of the Presence in the house of God because of hunger (1 Sam. 21:1–6). This episode gives Jesus a chance to announce that he is greater than the Temple, that God loves mercy more than sacrifice, and that the Son of Man is the lord of the Sabbath. To defend his decision to heal the man with a withered hand, he asks the Pharisees whether it is ethical to save a sheep that falls into the pit on the Sabbath, and how much more valuable a human being is than a sheep. So he declares that it is lawful to do something good on the Sabbath. In these two incidents, Jesus proves that he knows the scriptures even better than the Pharisees, and teaches that even the holiest law is meant to show God's mercy and to meet human needs. The law is a gift from God to benefit God's people in emergencies. One should not forget human plight while keeping the divine law. Silenced by Jesus' compelling argument, the Pharisees become enraged and decide to destroy him. Their injured pride becomes the root of all evils to come.

One of the most malicious charges they bring against Jesus is casting out demons in league with Beelzebub, their ruler, which is a deadly sin in biblical law and condemned in Deuteronomy. Although in Mark's gospel it is the "scribes from Jerusalem" who issue the indictment, in Matthew it is the "Pharisees" who twice accuse Jesus of doing exorcism through Beelzebul (9:34; 12:24). Jesus rebuts them with two rhetorical questions. If Satan casts out Satan, he is divided against himself; how then will his kingdom stand? If Jesus casts out demons by Beelzebul, by whom do the Pharisaic exorcists cast out demons? Moreover, Jesus warns them that because he has cast out demons by the Spirit of God, they need to bear in mind that "whoever speaks against the Holy Spirit will not be forgiven, either in this age or in the age to come" (12:32). Be cautious, Jesus is saying—angry language in heated debates has serious consequences beyond hurting relationship.

The Pharisees also complain against Jesus' disciples for not washing their hands before meals and thus breaking a purity law according to the so-called "tradition of the elders" (15:2). This controversy seems trivial, but Jesus takes it very seriously because the Pharisees are appealing to an authority other than Scripture. Thus he chastises them for honoring their sectarian oral tradition more than the commandment of God prescribed in the scriptures. They have, for instance, exempted people who have offered money to God from supporting their parents, even though honoring parents is stipulated in the Ten Commandments. Calling them "hypocrites," Jesus cites the prophet Isaiah to denounce their lip service to merely human precepts, and condemns them as "blind guides of the blind" (15:14). At this point of the story, Jesus has moved from well-reasoned self-defense to passionate chastisement of his opponents. It is not only their self-righteousness and arrogance, but also their hypocrisy and falsehood with which he now takes issue.

The tension between Jesus and the Pharisees escalates to full-blown hostility. On the journey to Jerusalem, some of the Pharisees come to test Jesus by pitching him against Moses on matters of divorce. Jesus makes a brilliant argument. Citing Genesis 2:24— "What God has joined together, let no one separate"—he upholds matrimony as the intimate relationship of God's own making that should be honored with fidelity. The certificate of divorce is a concession Moses was compelled to make because of the hard-heartedness of his rebellious people, and so Jesus forbids divorce except in cases of unchastity (19:9). Here again Jesus demonstrates his expertise in scriptural interpretation and wisdom on legal rulings. With his authority as the new Moses, Jesus overturns the Mosaic granting of easy divorce that is prejudicial against women and reminds his disciples of the sacred nature of marriage, whereby a man and a woman leave their parents to become united as one flesh. It is a covenant set up by God and ought to be honored with faithful commitment.

With his authority as the new Moses, Jesus overturns the Mosaic granting of easy divorce that is prejudicial against women and reminds his disciples of the sacred nature of marriage.

While Jesus is in Jerusalem, the Pharisees join with the chief priests to challenge his authority. When Jesus declares that the kingdom of God will be taken away from them, citing Psalm 118—"The stone that the builders rejected has become the chief cornerstone"—

to censure their stubbornness, they know Jesus is referring to them. As their final attempt to entrap him, then, they ask Jesus which commandment is the greatest in the law. There are over six hundred laws in Scripture and countless more in the traditions developed by the priests, Sadducees, and Pharisees, so that teachers of the law often debated with one another about which was the greatest and most foundational of all. Jesus' answer?

> "You shall love the Lord your God with all your heart, and with all your soul, and with all your mind." This is the greatest and first commandment. And a second is like it: "You shall love your neighbor as yourself." On these two commandments hang all the law and the prophets. (22:37–40)

These two commandments of love regulate both our vertical relationship with God and our horizontal relationship with others, covering every aspect of our lives and grounding our values and behaviors on the virtue of love. It is so simple and compelling that no one can argue against Jesus. From that day on, Matthew tells us, no one dare ask him any more questions.

Tracking Jesus' career, the Pharisees have taken many opportunities to complain, accuse, and entrap him wherever he travels. However, Jesus has always been able to justify his actions and explain his teachings by the authority of the scriptures and with compelling arguments. On matters of the law, in particular, he always prevails on his learned opponents. Besides showing how Jesus outwits his hostile opponents, the debates and conflicts often expose the Pharisees' ignorance. The stage is set for fresh confrontation.

In chapter 23 Jesus lashes out in frustration and fury, using harsh language against the Pharisees and the scribes without any reservation. It is a rare sight of Jesus in passionate rage, and we only see it elsewhere when he casts out the money changers from the Temple. Here Jesus denounces the Pharisees and the scribes with seven prophetic woes, calling them "hypocrites" and "blind guides" (23:13, 16). The term for "hypocrisy" in Greek language originated from a theatrical term, *hypocrites,* which means "playing a part on the stage," which refers to a mask or public façade that a person puts on for others to see. As Jesus uses the word, it connotes inconsistency, pretense, and dishonesty. The label of "blind guide" points to the Pharisees' incompetence and falsehood as teachers of the law.

In his denunciation against the Pharisees, Jesus focuses on three negative traits. First is their vanity and arrogance. They broaden their phylacteries and lengthen their fringes to show their piety. They desire the place of honor at banquets and the best seats in the synagogues, and want to be greeted with respect in marketplaces. Even though they conduct acts of piety, they love self-aggrandizement rather than the glory of God. Second, Jesus condemns their incompetence as teachers of the law. They do not love the kingdom of heaven and often prohibit others from entering it. They are interested in tithing mint, dill, and cumin, but pass over issues of justice, mercy, and faith, and do not teach people the matter of real importance before God. Third, they are greedy for money and self-indulgent in personal conduct, falsely accusing the prophets of God and persecuting the righteous who abide by the law.

Why does Matthew call special attention to the Pharisees as Jesus' archenemies? It may be true that the Pharisees in Palestine are particularly concerned about Jesus' radical interpretation of the law, which in their judgment may lead the people astray, so they take it upon themselves to challenge and discredit Jesus as teacher of the law at any cost. But Matthew has another reason to highlight their hostility. At the time that Matthew's gospel was composed, the rabbis who taught the law in the synagogues were the successors to the Pharisees in Jesus' time and major opponents to Matthew's church. They criticized Jesus and his followers as lawless and godless. Under the circumstances, the conflict stories offer not only historical information but contextual relevance to Matthew's readers.

At the time that Matthew's gospel was composed, the rabbis who taught the law in the synagogues were the successors to the Pharisees in Jesus' time and major opponents to Matthew's church.

Recalling the Pharisees' tense conflict with Jesus, Matthew may hope to accomplish three purposes. The first is apologetic. These debates and conflict stories illustrate Jesus' expertise in the scriptures and his wisdom in legal argument, so they can help Matthew's church defend its faith in Jesus against the false accusations of the rabbis. Jesus' answer to the Pharisees' charge against his friendly association with tax collectors and sinners, for instance, helps Matthew's church justify their inclusion of the Gentiles, whom the rabbis regard as unclean in the law, to be equal members of the kingdom of heaven with their Jewish brothers and sisters. Jesus' interpretation of the scriptures also explains why Matthew's church believe that Jesus' commandments clarify and fulfill God's will in the law and the prophets, and will be the criteria for the final judgment.

The second reason is polemical. Matthew's conflict stories diminish the credibility of the Pharisees as teachers of the law, because they reject Jesus out of jealousy and self-interest rather than out of righteousness. He calls them hypocrites and "blind guides," murderers and liars. These damaging claims are serious indictments against the rabbis of Matthew's time who, on a mission to consolidate their authority as synagogue leaders and restore the community life in the aftermath of the First Jewish War, may have aggressively harassed other dissident groups.

Jesus' comments on Sabbath, purity, and divorce, for instance, helped explain why Christians meet for worship on Sunday, ignore some ritualistic traditions, and do not allow easy divorce.

Finally, Matthew's purpose is didactic. The debates on matters of the law teach Matthew's readers a new way of life. Jesus' comments on Sabbath, purity, and divorce, for instance, help explain why Christians meet for worship on Sunday, ignore some ritualistic traditions, and do not allow easy divorce. Jesus' answer about the greatest of the laws, loving God and loving neighbor, summarizes for them in concrete terms God's will in the vast corpus of the Scripture and the traditions. Loving God and loving neighbors become the most important guidelines for the practice of Christian life.

The Chief Priests and Elders

While in Jerusalem, Jesus faces intensifying hostility from many directions. Besides his usual antagonists—the Pharisees and the scribes—a host of new enemies join the opposition. When Jesus preaches the gospel, teaches the law, and heals the sick in the Temple, he is immediately challenged by the chief priests and the elders: "By what authority are you doing these things, and who gave you this authority?" (21:23). These two groups of leaders possess a socially sanctioned authority to oversee religious and civil matters of the Jewish people through the offices of the Temple and the Sanhedrin, so they consider it their prerogative to question the legitimacy of Jesus' claim to authority as he conducts audacious activities in the name of the kingdom of heaven. In reply, Jesus asks them an unanswerable question about the authority of the well-respected preacher John the Baptist, who has inspired a revival movement among pious people:

> "Did the baptism of John come from heaven, or was it of human origin?" And they argued with one another, "If we say, 'From heaven,' he will say to us, 'Why then did you not believe him?' But if we say, 'Of human origin,' we are afraid of the crowd; for all regard John as a prophet." So they answered Jesus, "We do not know." And he said to them, "Neither will I tell you by what authority I am doing these things." (21:25–27)

Jesus knows that they are reluctant to acknowledge John's prophetic authority, which summons people to change their minds and lives. Like John's, Jesus' authority is radically different from that of the chief priests and the elders; it subverts the historical tradition and the status quo. His healing power and his radical teaching have the power to change minds, hearts, values, and the systems of the world as they know it, while his wisdom silences even his most learned rivals. Acting with compassion and speaking with authority as the Son of God, he thoroughly unnerves the privileged elites in Jerusalem. But Jesus refuses to tell them where exactly his authority comes from. Why? If the chief priests and the elders are unwilling to acknowledge John the Baptist's prophetic authority, which has transformed so many lives, surely they are not going to accept Jesus' divine authority. They refuse to accept him; they do not want to share with him their authority over the community.

It is to unmask these leaders' stubborn rejection of Jesus and to warn them about the horrendous consequences of their decision that Jesus tells three parables (21:28–22:14). These parables are followed by questions and answers that invite his hearers to interpret them allegorically and thus connect the characters in the parables to the chief priests and the elders. The parable of the two sons is very short. The first son refuses to work in his father's vineyard, but later regrets his decision and goes, while the second son promises to go but does not. Then Jesus asks, "Which of the two did the will of his father?" (21:31). When the chief priests and the elders reply, "The first," Jesus identifies the good son with the tax collectors and the prostitutes because they have listened to John the Baptist and turned their lives around. They will enter the kingdom of heaven, Jesus declares, but the chief priests and the elders will not—like the second son, they pay only lip service to God.

The parable of the wicked tenants is based on the well-known parable of the vineyard in the prophecy of Isaiah. A landowner plants a vineyard, puts a fence around it, digs a wine press, and builds a watchtower before leasing it out to his tenants. At harvest time he sends his slaves to collect his produce, but the tenants refuse to pay their due. Worse yet, they seize, beat, kill, and stone the slaves. Jesus' audience and Matthew's readers would recognize that, as Isaiah interprets the story, the owner represents God, the vineyard Israel, and the tenants their kings and priests. In Isaiah 5, this parable is a story of how God's efforts to provide abundantly for the people of Israel prove futile— the harvest yields only sour grapes—because of the arrogance and injustices of Israel's leaders. It is an oracle of judgment against the people of God and foreshadows the siege against Israel by the Assyrian armies, ending in capture and enslavement. The covenant with God has been broken, and this is the punishment.

> *Jesus' audience and Matthew's readers would recognize that, as Isaiah interprets the story, the owner represents God, the vineyard Israel, and the tenants their kings and priests.*

In Matthew's extended version of the parable, Jesus emphasizes God's patience by adding a new element. The owner of the vineyard sends his own son to collect the harvest, but to no avail—conspiring to steal his inheritance, the tenants kill the son and throw him out of the vineyard. What should the owner do to these wicked tenants? Jesus asks. The chief priests and the elders reply that those murderous tenants should be put to death and the vineyard leased to others. Hearing that, Jesus condemns them: "Therefore I tell you, the kingdom of God will be taken away from you and given to a people that produces the fruits of the kingdom" (21:43). The chief priests now understand that Jesus is speaking of them, and they want to arrest him, "but they feared the crowds, because they regarded him as a prophet" (21:46). The chief priests and the elders know that Jesus is condemning them as the wicked tenants, and they harden their hearts. Then Jesus tells them one more parable.

A king plans a banquet for his son's wedding, and when the date of celebration draws near, he sends his slaves to remind his invited guests to come. But the guests offer many excuses and make light of the invitation; some even seize, mistreat, and kill the king's slaves. Outraged by his insolent subjects, the king sends his troops to destroy those murderers and burn their city. Then, in order to fill his banquet hall, the king sends his slaves out to the streets to invite everyone—"both good and bad"—to attend the banquet.

To Matthew's earliest readers, this would have been a horrifying story. Living as they did at the end of the first century, they would have been shocked to see certain key details of the parable fulfilled in the recent destruction of Jerusalem in 70 CE. They would have perceived that the king represented God, his son Jesus Christ, and the wedding banquet the joyful celebration of messianic salvation. The first invited guests, who insult the king and persecute his servants, are those religious elites who are held responsible for the fall of the holy city. The guests invited from the streets are understood to be the Gentile Christians who enter the banquet later, by grace. Read allegorically, with the ruins of Jerusalem in sight, this parable would certainly cause Matthew's readers, both Jewish and Gentile, to reflect somberly on God's salvation and judgment. Rebellion against God causes the downfall of the holy city, now the second time in history; so everybody must repent before God.

Regrettably, some Christian interpreters in later centuries began to misread this parable as an allegory of condemnation against all Jewish people and use it to justify anti-Semitism. As an ironic consequence, Christians became the villains of the parable, the first invited guests who rejected God's grace and persecuted God's people. Anti-Semitic interpretation of the parable is wrong not only on theological ground or by moral standard, but also exegetically. It is important to remember that, unlike its Lukan parallel, Matthew's parable does not end on a happy note—a man who arrives without the proper wedding clothes is thrown out of the banquet and punished when the king arrives. Why does Matthew add this scene? Is the king's judgment fair? How can one reasonably expect a man from the streets to carry a wedding robe with him? How do we answer these questions?

In the first place, the parable concerns God's dealing with the Christians rather than the Jews; the new guests can abuse God's free offer of grace just as the first guests do. So Matthew wants to forewarn his Gentile readers that without a wedding robe, they may be cast out of God's kingdom in the final judgment. Jesus has issued the same warning at the end of the Sermon on the Mount: "Not everyone who says to me, 'Lord, Lord,' will enter the kingdom of heaven, but only the one who does the will of my Father in heaven" (7:21).

What then does the wedding robe symbolize? In the history of interpretation, many suggestions have been proposed. John Chrysostom interpreted it as righteousness; Augustine took it to mean charity, while for Luther it meant faith in Christ. These interpretations may all be partially right, but they reflect more of the interpreters' theology than Matthew's insights. If we try to interpret it within Matthew's symbolic world, the possible meaning of the wedding robe can be found in the prophet Isaiah, whom Matthew cites frequently in his gospel:

> I will greatly rejoice in the LORD,
> my whole being shall exult in my God;
> for he has clothed me with the garments of salvation,
> he has covered me with the robe of righteousness,
> as a bridegroom decks himself with a garland,
> and as a bride adorns herself with her jewels. (Isa. 61:10)

According to Isaiah, the wedding robe refers to the divine grace of salvation and the human life of righteousness; both are possible, Matthew would suggest, by accepting and following Jesus Christ. It is true that the parable of the wedding banquet is a prophetic indictment against the chief priests and the elders, showing how their rejection of Jesus, the Son of God, amounts to a rebellion against God and the Messiah. They are thus held liable for the terrible consequences. The surprising ending of the parable, however, shows that Matthew's ultimate concern is not to assign historical blame for the destruction of Jerusalem, but to issue a serious warning to his readers about the final judgment. Christians enter the kingdom of heaven by grace, but they must remember that they need both the garment of salvation and the robe of righteousness to survive the final judgment. For Matthew, therefore, the parable serves as an admonition for the church rather than an accusation against the synagogue. Thus, he ends the parable with another saying of Jesus: "For many are called, but few are chosen" (22:14). Membership in the church does not guarantee survival in the final reckoning with God.

The surprising ending of the parable, however, shows that Matthew is not assigning blame for the destruction of Jerusalem, but to issuing a serious warning to his readers about the final judgment.

Besides the chief priests and the elders, Jesus is also bombarded by many other religious leaders who want to test and discredit him. The politically well-connected Herodians attempt to trick him with a question about paying taxes to Caesar. If Jesus says it is indeed lawful, then he will lose his credibility as a prophet and favor with his Jewish followers. If he says it is not lawful, he can be charged before the Roman authorities for treason. Deconstructing their either-or choices, Jesus' answer—"Give therefore to the emperor the things that are the emperors, and to God the things that are God's" (22:21)—is politically savvy and theologically sound. No one can accuse him of treason against Caesar, yet he is saying one should honor God with the utmost loyalty because everything belongs to God. This wise answer saves him from political entrapment.

The more liberal Sadducees ask Jesus another kind of question, hoping to trick him into denying the resurrection. If a woman marries seven brothers in succession, all of whom die, which brother will be her husband at the resurrection? Thus they try to pitch the levirate marriage law of Moses, whereby widows were to remarry within the family, against the idea of resurrection. Refusing to be ensnared by this false dichotomy, Jesus appeals to the higher power of God beyond human logic to argue that at the resurrection we will be like angels in heaven, not bound by the relationship of husband and wife, and that the God of the living can easily bring life beyond death.

Finally, a lawyer tests Jesus by asking him which commandment is the greatest. Jesus wins his approval when he replies that the greatest and the first is, "You shall love the Lord your God with all your heart, and with all your soul, and with all your mind," and the second, "You shall love your neighbor as yourself," because on these two commandments "hang all the law and the prophets" (22:40). These three rounds of verbal jousting show how much wiser Jesus is than all his opponents. He proves to be an expert teacher of God's will who knows the doctrine, the law, and the scriptures. These tests would boost the confidence of Matthew's community in Jesus Christ as their Lord when they faced challenges from their opponents from the synagogue in Antioch.

Since no one can find fault with Jesus' teaching, the chief priests and the elders finally resort to false testimony. They arrest him by force and put him on trial before Caiaphas the high priest. They look for false witness but cannot find one that would stand. Two people accuse him of attempting to destroy the Temple, but Jesus keeps silent during the interrogation. Not until Caiaphas asks him whether he is the Messiah, the Son of God, does Jesus admit it implicitly by answering: "You have said so" (26:64). At once, the Sanhedrin convicts him of blasphemy and sentences him to the death penalty. This trial is a dramatic expression of the conflict between Jesus and the leaders in Jerusalem. The underhanded way in which the high priest conducts himself shows how malicious Jesus' opponents are, as the conflict between light and darkness reaches the point of life and death.

Pilate the Roman Governor

The chief priests and the elders have no authority under Roman rule to execute, so they bind Jesus and hand him over to Pilate, the Roman governor. They need to persuade Pilate that Jesus deserves to die, so another trial is held. When Pilate asks Jesus whether he is the "king of the Jews," again Jesus implies it is true: "You say so" (27:11). But he refuses to reply to any charges from the chief priests and the elders. Pilate knows that their accusation of Jesus comes out of jealousy rather than credible evidence, so he tries to release Jesus by citing the custom of amnesty for one criminal at Passover. But the chief priests and the elders incite the crowds to ask for Barabbas to be freed instead, and call for Jesus' death. Under the pressure of a brewing riot, Pilate gives in to their demand. Even though he washes his hands before the crowd to show his innocence, he has not upheld the justice that his office requires of him. Lending his political authority to crucify Jesus, Pilate becomes a reluctant but undeniable accomplice to a scheme that he knows is wrong.

One troubling comment on the trial of Jesus has made an enormous impact in the history of interpretation and had grave consequences for Jewish-Christian relationship. As the narrator, Matthew comments: "Then the people as a whole [*pas ho laos*] answered, 'His blood be on us and on our children!'" (27:25). Note that the Greek word for "people" in this verse is not *oxlos* (crowds), referring to the people present at the trial (27:20), but *laos* (people), which can mean the general public, a nation, or the people of God, and thus implies the whole Jewish people. The word *pas* ("all," "as a whole") further emphasizes that all people in this ethnic group are unanimous in calling for Jesus' death. To swear a curse of blood on oneself shows that one accepts full responsibility for a person's death. Thus Matthew's comment in 27:25 reads as if the whole Jewish people are so intent on killing Jesus that they are willing to risk their own lives and that of their offspring with a curse before the eternal God. In light of Jerusalem's destruction in 70 CE, many Christian interpreters believed that this self-incriminating curse was fulfilled in the First Jewish War. Furthermore, because all Jews are believed to have cursed themselves on Jesus' death, some later interpreters took one step further and used this verse as a justification for anti-Semitism. Indeed, by saying "all the people" instead of "the crowds," Matthew seems to have implicated all the Jews in rejecting Jesus—but does he mean to say that the whole Jewish people will be condemned forever? Can his story of the trial be used to support anti-Semitism? No, Matthew does not believe the whole Jewish people will be condemned, nor should ethnic discrimination or religious bigotry be permitted.

The first reason has to do with his ethnic identity. Matthew himself is Jewish and many members of his church are Jewish, so there is no reason and no basis for him to be anti-Semitic or anti-Jewish in the narrow sense of "ethno-phobia." The second reason has to do with his religious understanding. Even though Matthew is passionately debating with the Pharisaic rabbis and the rulers of the synagogues over his faith in Jesus as the Christ, he

Even though Matthew is passionately debating with the Pharisaic rabbis and the rulers of the synagogues over his faith in Jesus as the Christ, he believes that God remains faithful to "the lost sheep" of the house of Israel.

believes that God remains faithful to the covenant and "the lost sheep" of the house of Israel.For Jesus has called disciples and attracted followers mainly from among the Jews, and the disciples are commissioned to make disciples of "all nations," which includes the Jews. For him, the new "people" to inherit the kingdom of heaven is defined by the fruits of righteousness, not by ethnicity of any kind. Both the Jews and the Gentiles are welcome to the wedding banquet.

The last and most fundamental reason is exegetical. I will argue that Matthew understands "all the people" and the "curse of blood" in light of the prophet Jeremiah's Temple sermon and his trial by the priests in 609 BCE (Jer. 26:1–24). In that sermon Jeremiah condemned the cities of Judah, prophesying that because they did not walk in the law of God, God will lay waste to the Temple and make Jerusalem a curse for all the nations of the earth. The priests, prophets, and "all the people" were enraged by Jeremiah's oracle of judgment, and at his trial claimed that he deserved the sentence of death for prophesying against the holy city. In response to the charge, Jeremiah said, "Only know for certain that if you put me to death, you will be bringing innocent blood upon yourselves and upon this city and its inhabitants, for in truth the LORD sent me to you to speak all these words in your ears." After hearing Jeremiah, the officials and all the people (*pas ho laos*) said to the priests and the prophets, "This man does not deserve the sentence of death, for he has spoken to us in the name of the LORD our God" (26:14–16).

There are striking parallels with Jesus' trial: the priests and the prophets (the elders), the officials (Pilate), charge of blasphemy against the holy city, sentence of death, innocent blood, the curse of blood, and the use of the phrase "all the people." But there is also a sharp contrast in the final verdict. In writing of "all the people" swearing the "curse of blood" before Pilate, therefore, Matthew is trying to evoke the story of Jeremiah's trial for comparison in order to make the point that Jesus is innocent and his accusers are malicious. Perhaps Matthew is hoping for all the people of God in his time to repent and accept Jesus. With this allusion, Matthew may also be suggesting that the destruction of Jerusalem is a divine discipline and not a punishment, so that the people of God may change their lives and return to receive God's blessings again. In other words,

Matthew's purpose is to link Jesus' trial to Jeremiah's, not to condemn an entire ethnic group nor to justify any discrimination against the Jews. As far as Matthew is concerned, the lesson to be learned from Jesus' trial is that *all* people would be wise to recognize Jesus as the Messiah and the Son of God, whose innocent blood is shed for the forgiveness of sins.

Having been sentenced to death, Jesus is tortured by the Roman soldiers and mocked by the spectators. It is significant that on the cross he is officially charged as "the King of the Jews," which echoes the title the wise men from the East use when seeking the infant Jesus: "Where is the child who has been born king of the Jews?" From birth to death, the story of conflict thus comes to a circle. Jesus faces the same political forces of the empire that cannot tolerate any possible threat to its clutch to power and does not hesitate to use violence to eradicate any potential challengers. However, the outcome of both stories show that Jesus is safely brought to safety in Egypt for a few years and then is triumphantly raised from the dead in three days. Even the most

> On the cross Jesus is officially charged as "the King of the Jews," which echoes the title the wise men from the East use when seeking the infant Jesus: "Where is the child who has been born king of the Jews?"

powerful empire on earth cannot thwart God's plan for salvation nor endanger God's Son. This is the conviction that sustained the faith and mission of Matthew and the early church as they faced persecution by the Roman Empire.

This chapter has shown that Jesus was tested and assaulted by many learned and powerful opponents. The Pharisees and the chief priests led a coalition of leaders to question his teaching of the law, denied his authority to exorcise, and accused him of blasphemy. His self-possessed authority as the new Moses and his radical teaching on the kingdom of heaven were considered serious threats to the established tradition of the law, so they constantly tried to discredit him and discourage his followers. In the political realm, he was vulnerable to the power of the Roman Empire. As "the king of the Jews" Jesus was regarded as a potential risk to the security and order of the empire, so he was put to death on the cross. In the spiritual realm, the devil was his greatest opponent, tempting him with false promises. Because Jesus ushered in the kingdom of heaven and began to disarm the evil powers that cripple human body and soul, the devil tried to seduce him in the desert, on the mountaintop, and in the garden of Gethsemane. Many followers of Jesus in the world today also face all sorts of opposition and temptation in daily life. Some of them are persecuted and jailed by the power of the state because they confess to be Christians; others are ostracized by their families and communities because they profess faith in Jesus. Still others have to struggle with oppressive traditions, confusing ideologies, and strong cultural pressures if they want to live as faithful disciples of Jesus. And all Christians have to make decisions about their loyalties, priorities, and choices every day to bear witness to their faith.

What is encouraging is that Jesus was always able to defeat his opponents. Against a stronger wind, the kite flies higher; on a towering wave, the surfer glides farther. These conflict stories vividly demonstrate Jesus' absolute loyalty to God, his spiritual integrity, and his extraordinary wisdom. They set a good example for us to serve as bold witnesses and prophetic voices for justice and love in a world that worships power and profits. In other words, the conflict stories reveal Jesus' traits of character that we, as his disciples, can learn by imitation, for what is remarkable about Matthew's story is how Jesus uses his indictments against the Pharisees and the chief priests to serve as warnings for his disciples. Even from their persecutors, they can learn something important about God and about the right way of life.

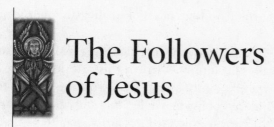

CHAPTER FIVE

The Followers of Jesus

In Asia, where Buddhism, Hinduism, Islam, and folk religions are traditional and dominant faiths, Christianity is a late comer and considered a foreign religion. Except in the Philippines and Korea, native people who have converted to Christianity are minorities and often despised as cultural traitors and social agitators. Christians in Asia tend to form a closely knit social group to support each other, but their relationship with the community at large is often strenuous and tense. Their personal beliefs may be tolerated, but their behaviors are always under scrutiny. From time to time, Christian doctrine might be of interest to some scholars, but moral excellence is the only way for churches to show that Christianity is benevolent and valid. Christian faith emphasizes the love of God and the change of life—to potential converts, these are the two most attractive ideas. Yet not all Christians are as forgiving, loving, and generous as they should be, so their opponents can say, "If Christians go to heaven, I would rather go to hell." There cannot be any stronger indictment than this, and it indicates the critical importance of Christian identity and character. Whatever Christians claim to be, if they do not live up to the standard Jesus has spoken, they dishonor themselves and their God.

In Europe and North America, Christians face a similar challenge because they live in cultures where the historical influence of Christian faith is rapidly diminishing. Secularization pushes the Judeo-Christian God into oblivion, while postmodernism declares traditional values and norms outdated. Is Christian faith still relevant? Is it necessary to believe in God? Why do we need Jesus? What is the value of the church? Does Christian faith have any say on our way of life? What difference does it make? These questions point to the vital importance of Christian identity and character as well.

What does it mean to be Christian? Does it refer to someone who believes in Jesus as Christ and the Son of God as defined in traditional doctrines, or someone who practices Jesus' moral teaching of love in the family, workplace, and society? Is a Christian someone who joins the church and participates in its worship, or someone who is fascinated by Jesus and studies his ideas? Whatever definition we choose, two fundamental questions are important to raise. What makes a Christian different? Why does anyone want to be a Christian? Once we are clear about Christian identity, we will be able to know how to behave accordingly.

People become Christians for different reasons. Some encounter Jesus as the Son of God through religious experiences such as prayers and miracles; they are converted. Others become curious about Jesus because of his teaching and his impact on followers; they decide to find out more. Still others simply come along to get along with their families or friends in the church; it does not hurt to belong to a close community. Each Christian may have a personal reason to convert or to join the church, but all will have to grow deeper in their understanding and stronger in their faith, because becoming Christian involves a continuous change of heart and mind. It is not an easy path. We know that Jesus promises his followers many blessings of God, including the forgiveness of sins and eternal life, but he also demands they live up to a high standard of spiritual, moral, and social life. Jesus' kingdom of heaven does not belong to this world, so following him often means clashing with common assumptions and popular expectations, risking alienation or ostracism. Therefore

Jesus' followers have to be totally committed to his vision and be willing to obey his commandments. To walk with Jesus in their daily life, they need to ask, "What would Jesus do?" It is not enough to believe in Jesus' name or to admire his teaching. They have to think and behave like him; that is to say, to become his disciples.

> *It is not enough to believe in Jesus' name or to admire his teaching. They have to think and behave like him; that is to say, to become his disciples.*

Jesus' Followers

In his gospel, not only does Matthew present stories of Jesus' followers and disciples, but concludes it with the Great Commission with which Jesus bids them to "make disciples of all nations" (28:19). What does Matthew have to say about the disciples and the idea of discipleship?

Jesus is a man of charisma. He proclaims the coming of the kingdom of heaven with confidence, teaches the Sermon on the Mount with authority, and heals the sick and the possessed with power, so he attracts a big following wherever he travels. Is he a prophet like Elijah or Jeremiah? The curious gather around to hear him teach and see him perform miracles at home or in the street, while the suffering approach him for healing and comfort day and night. The hungry want to make him their king after he feeds them with five loaves and two fish; the angry crowds at Pilate's court side with their chief priests and elders to demand his crucifixion. To all Jesus shows compassion, as a shepherd cares for his flock of sheep, and summons them to follow him:

> Come to me, all you that are weary and are carrying heavy burdens,
> and I will give you rest. Take my yoke upon you, and learn from me; for
> I am gentle and humble in heart, and you will find rest for your souls.
> For my yoke is easy, and my burden is light. (11:28–30)

Yet most of the crowds around Jesus do not respond to him in kind; their loyalty swings back and forth. Only a few are so moved and touched by Jesus that they do step forward to become his followers. Most of his followers are anonymous, but their life-transforming encounters with Jesus are reported in Matthew's gospel with important messages to the readers.

One of the early examples is a Roman centurion in Capernaum, who pleads with Jesus to cure his servant of paralysis. When Jesus offers to go to his house, the centurion says he is not worth Jesus' trouble and believes that Jesus can cure his servant by simply speaking a word. This centurion is remarkable, a caring master who also humbles himself before Jesus even though he is a man of authority. He may be trying to save Jesus from the dilemma of entering a Gentile's house at the risk of becoming ritually unclean, but most importantly, he shows an extraordinary faith in Jesus' power to heal the sick even from a distance. No wonder that Jesus himself is amazed, saying to those who follow him: "Truly I tell you, in no one in Israel have I found such faith" (8:10). This miracle story becomes a paradigm tale, for as a result of his faith, his servant is cured. He becomes a model of faith for Jesus' followers as well as a herald for the Gentiles "from east and west" who "will eat with Abraham and Isaac and Jacob in the kingdom of heaven" (8:11). His virtues of love, humility, and faith are highlighted to shame the rebellious "heirs of the kingdom" into repentance. For Matthew, this follower of Jesus serves two purposes for his readers, both didactic and polemical.

> *The centurion becomes a model of faith for Jesus' followers as well as a herald for the Gentiles "from east and west" who "will eat with Abraham and Isaac and Jacob in the kingdom of heaven" (8:11).*

Another remarkable example is the Canaanite mother in Tyre and Sidon area whose story we have discussed in Chapter Three. This Gentile woman demonstrates the character of love, persistence, humility, and faith that changes Jesus' mind and outshines everyone else (15:28).

The two blind men outside of Jericho whom Jesus heals provide yet one more example of Jesus' ability to draw people to him. Sitting by the roadside, they hear that Jesus is passing by and call out for mercy. The crowd sternly orders them to be quiet, but they shout for Jesus' attention all the more. Hearing their persistent cry,

> Jesus stood still and called them, saying, "What do you want me to do for you?" They said to him, "Lord, let our eyes be opened." Moved with compassion, Jesus touched their eyes. Immediately they regained their sight and followed him. (20:32–34)

These two blind men persistently ask for help from Jesus, even though the crowd try to hush them. Like the Roman centurion, they humbly and sincerely call Jesus "Lord" and thus move him to compassion. It is noteworthy that, as soon as they are cured, they become Jesus' followers. They follow him into Jerusalem where he will be betrayed, tortured, and crucified.

All the followers of Jesus exhibit three remarkable traits, and the first of these is love. Those who become his disciples love their friends, families, and themselves. Their love is so strong that they persevere even when their request for help is denied or thwarted, proving that love can overcome any barriers that might stand between God's blessing and human need. The second quality they share is humility. They call Jesus "*kyrios*" (Lord), an honorific term in Greek referring to a person of higher social standing, such as an overlord, superior, or king. In the Septuagint, which is the Greek translation of the Old Testament, it is also used to translate the Hebrew word "*Adonai*" (Lord) for God. Calling Jesus "Lord" is thus a clear indication of their recognition of Jesus' superiority and may even be a confession of his divinity. They know they are in need and Jesus the Lord can help.

Last of all, they have faith. They believe strongly in Jesus' healing power. The centurion's desire for Jesus simply to speak a word without visiting the paralyzed servant shows an incredible faith in Jesus' authority over diseases, as does the two blind men's struggle to be heard. Persistent love, humble submission, and undeterred faith characterize these followers of Jesus and explain why they are able to experience the miracles of healing. These followers also come from the fringe of the society, a foreigner and two blind men. They are the despised, the downtrodden, and the invalid, yet turn out to be the ones who receive Jesus' healings and become his followers. Their desperation may have led them to recognize their frailty and rely on Jesus' compassion, but their faith in Jesus enables them to receive God's grace. Their humble submission to Jesus begins a new relationship; their purpose in life now rests in the service of Jesus Christ as their Lord.

Jesus' Disciples

Matthew provides a biography of Jesus from birth to death and resurrection. He tells us how extraordinary Jesus is, what remarkable things he has taught and done, and how significant he is to all people in the world. At the same time, Matthew depicts how often Jesus astonishes the crowds, how he attracts his followers, and how hard he tries to train the twelve disciples. Among the characters in the story, it may be safe to assume that most readers will identify themselves with the disciples as they follow and interact with Jesus from Galilee to Jerusalem. As New Testament scholar Ulrich Luz argues, there is a "transparency" between the disciples in the text and the readers in front of the text.[1] Christian readers will find a particular rapport with the disciples and read their stories as their own. In his lifetime, Jesus may have called only a small group of followers in Galilee to be his disciples, but after his resurrection he commanded that all believers be baptized and all the baptized be trained in his teaching to become his disciples. Thus everything we learn about disciples and discipleship in the gospel applies to Matthew's own community and to us today.

In the first place, notice how Jesus chooses and calls his disciples. In response to Jesus' shocking teaching and miracles, some people from the bystanding crowds recognize him as a prophet and become his followers. It is from among these few that Jesus calls twelve men to leave their families and livelihoods to become his disciples. This is different from many other teachers of his time. Greek and Roman philosophers, such as the Stoics and the Epicureans, established schools in the cities to teach physics, logics, rhetoric, and moral principles to students who could afford to pay tuitions and fees. Pharisaic rabbis sat in their homes or yeshivas to teach the law to students who have decided on their own to come and study with them. But Jesus is an itinerant teacher who travels from place to place and takes the initiative himself, while some who wish to become his disciples are discouraged. To a scribe who wishes to join Jesus' disciples, for instance, Jesus says, "Foxes have holes, and birds of the air have nests; but the Son of Man has nowhere to lay his head" (8:20). To another, who wants to go home first to bury his father, Jesus says: "Let the dead bury their own dead" (8:22). Becoming Jesus' disciples is not a personal choice, but a special call. It is Jesus who decides who he wants to call. Thus, discipleship means, first and foremost, honoring Jesus' prerogative. It is a privilege from God, not a choice of our own.

Why does Jesus choose twelve in number? For Matthew and his community, numbers had significance in their symbolic world, for they were believed to be one more way God revealed heavenly mysteries to God's servants. In the genealogy of Jesus, for instance, Matthew emphasizes the fourteen generations that existed between Abraham and David, David and the exile to Babylon, and the exile to Babylon and the Messiah. These historical figures are meant to remind his readers of the highpoints of God's intervention in Jewish history: election (the covenant with Abraham), unification (the kingdom of David), discipline (the exile to Babylon), and redemption (the coming of the Messiah). Fourteen, the number of generations in the intervals, is seven twice over, and seven is believed to be a perfect number. One way to understand the symbolism is that God created the world in six days and rested on the seventh. Another way to interpret it is to see number seven as the total of three and four—three representing heaven, earth, and underworld, while four represents the four directions: east, west, south, and north. In biblical cosmology, the three spheres and the four directions combine the vertical and the horizontal of space to make up the whole universe. For the same symbolic reason, Jesus tells Peter to forgive his brother seventy-seven (or seventy times seven) times to emphasize complete forgiveness, given over and over. It is no accident, either, that Matthew puts together seven woes against the Pharisees and the scribes to signal total condemnation against their sins of hypocrisy and wickedness.

For Matthew and his community, numbers had significance in their symbolic world, for they were believed to be one more way God revealed heavenly mysteries to God's servants.

What is the symbolic meaning of the number twelve? There are twelve months in a year and there were twelve tribes of the people of Israel. Because Jesus' ministry is to call the house of Israel to repent, calling twelve disciples to accompany him may be a prophetic sign of the creation of a new Israel, the new people to whom the kingdom of heaven will be given and from whom the fruits of the kingdom will be expected (21:43). This symbolic meaning is confirmed when Jesus declares to his disciples:

> Truly I tell you, at the renewal of all things, when the Son of Man is seated on the throne of his glory, you who have followed me will also sit on twelve thrones, judging the twelve tribes of Israel. (19:28)

With this saying Jesus promises his twelve disciples the authority to judge the people of Israel. What a privilege! It bestows enormous honor and status on the twelve disciples who, with the exception of Judas, become the holy apostles of the church, but what does it say about the people of Israel? How do we make sense of this polemic? Considering the historical context of his church, I think Matthew is recalling this saying of Jesus in order to issue a warning against opponents in the synagogues who, in his view, defied God's will when they persecuted Jesus' followers. He also provides it as comfort, a way of encouraging the persecuted Christians to hold on to their faith in Jesus—God will render judgment against their persecutors in the end. It is important to remember that, even in the most heated polemic, Matthew leaves the judgment to God in the future, when the Son of Man will come to preside over the final trial. Yes, the twelve disciples will receive the authority to advocate justice, but the final judgment belongs to the Son.

Even more important, furthermore, is the way Matthew concludes Jesus' conversation on this saying. Anyone who gives up everything to follow Jesus, as the twelve disciples have done, will inherit eternal life: "But many who are first will be last, and the last will be first" (19:30). For Matthew, the twelve disciples are spiritual models, but even they will sin, stumble, and fall behind. The judging of the twelve tribes of Israel is, therefore, to be understood as a warning for all the people of God, not as a prophecy that the church will in some way replace Israel.

> The judging of the twelve tribes of Israel is, therefore, to be understood as a warning for all the people of God, not as a prophecy that the church will in some way replace Israel.

Another question we must ask is this: why do the twelve answer Jesus' call? Why are they willing to give up everything to follow him? It is noteworthy that in no calling stories has Matthew mentioned their reasons for following him, nor does the gospel describe any struggle to make the right decision. A hint of their motivation may be detected from two incidents, however. In the first, a rich young man asks Jesus what he should do in order to have eternal life. After Jesus tells him to sell his possessions, give the money to the poor, and follow him, the young man goes away deeply grieved. When Jesus tells his followers how hard it is for a rich person to enter the kingdom of heaven, Peter asks Jesus what reward they will receive for leaving everything to follow him. Based on Peter's question, it seems that the disciples do hope to receive something for their sacrifice. What do they expect?

The second incident may yield a clue. On the way to Jerusalem, the disciples argue among themselves as to who is the greater, and the mother of John and James pleads for her sons to sit at Jesus' right and left when he becomes the messianic king. From this it seems that the twelve disciples are not innocent of ambition after all. They have obviously misunderstood Jesus' kingdom of heaven as an earthly regime, and he has to tell them repeatedly that in his kingdom anyone who wishes to be great shall be the servant of all. He himself must go to Jerusalem, undergo great suffering, and be killed. Thus it follows:

> If any want to become my followers, let them deny themselves and take up their cross and follow me. For those who want to save their life will lose it, and those who lose their life for my sake will find it. (16:24–25)

The enjoyment of power and honors is not the reason for becoming Jesus' disciples, because what he promises is suffering and death for his sake before they can receive the rewards of eternal life and the glory of the heavenly thrones. As theologian Dietrich Bonhoeffer has insightfully said:

> When Christ calls a man, he bids him to come and die. It may be a death like that of the first disciples who have to leave home and work to follow him, or it may be a death like Luther's, who had to leave the monastery and go out into the world. But it is the same death every time—death in Jesus Christ, the death of the old man at his call.[2]

In spite of this promise of sufferings to come, the twelve disciples still hold a position of privilege among Jesus' followers. By accompanying Jesus on his journey, they are able to hear his thought-provoking teachings about the way of righteousness and witness firsthand his powerful miracles that change people's lives. Their classroom is on the road. Jesus also gives them private instructions when the crowds disperse. He engages them in personal conversation and takes time to explain to them the mystery of the kingdom of heaven in parables, the will of God in the law and the prophets, the new way of life for the church, and the serious consequences of the final judgment. Yet these disciples are not merely students of religious knowledge, for they are also privileged to form an intimate relationship with Jesus, becoming his family members. In one instance, when people tell Jesus that his mother and siblings have come to see him, he responds with a question: "Who is my mother? And who are my brothers?" Pointing to his disciples, he then says, "Here are my mother and my brothers! For whoever does the will of my Father in heaven is my brother and sister and mother" (12:49–50). Disciples are thus defined as those who fulfill the will of God and enjoy an intimate, even familial relationship with Jesus. According to New Testament scholar Martin Hengel, the intimate personal relationship between Jesus and his disciples is a unique characteristic not found in philosophical schools or religious groups.[3]

Even so, the twelve disciples are flawed. They are earnest students who do not hesitate to ask Jesus to clarify his points or answer their questions, but from time to time they are chastised for their lack of understanding. For instance, on one occasion the Pharisees accuse the disciples of violating the tradition of the elders because they do not wash their hands before they eat. Jesus repudiates the Pharisees as hypocrites because they respect human tradition more than the word of God, insisting on the law of hand-washing but ignoring the commandment to provide for their parents. He also calls them "blind guides" who teach error, for it is not what goes into the mouth that defiles a person, but what comes out. The disciples do not understand what he means, so Jesus says in disappointment: "Are you also still without understanding?" (15:16).

At times, the disciples also lack faith and courage. Although they have already seen Jesus to be a miracle worker, when they are caught in a storm on the sea at night they are terrified even though Jesus is in the boat with them. He chastises them, "Why are you afraid, you of little faith?" (8:26). At the end of his life, Peter, John, and James fall asleep in fatigue when Jesus needs them to pray with him in the garden of Gethsemane, and all of them desert him in panic when he is arrested. Judas betrays Jesus for money and Peter denies him in public out of fear. Even when they meet the resurrected Jesus on the mountain and worship him, some are still in doubt. As such, the twelve disciples are not saints, but vulnerable human beings like the rest of us. Nevertheless, the risen Jesus trusts them enough to give them his great commission—the responsibility to make disciples of all nations. Furthermore, there is an even bigger surprise in store after Matthew's gospel has ended. We learn from the book of Acts that these flawed disciples were reinvigorated by

> *Discipleship is a holy calling that comes with the privilege of relating to Jesus, learning from him, and hearing his promises, but it is a journey of love that leads to the cross.*

the Holy Spirit to testify boldly to the resurrection of Jesus and convert many believers to establish the church. Reading their stories, we are reassured of God's amazing grace: we may be broken vessels, but the gracious God can always sanctify and mend us to serve the good purposes of the kingdom.

In brief, discipleship is a holy calling that comes with the privilege of relating to Jesus, learning from him, and hearing his promises of great rewards in eternity, but it is no easy task. Discipleship is a journey of love that leads to the cross. Jesus' mission is to proclaim the kingdom of heaven, to show mercy, to do righteousness, to heal the sick, to cast out demons, to debate the opponents, and to die on the cross for the sinners. The same is true for the disciples, who are called to learn from him, imitate him, and become his family. Discipleship is the process of constant conversion, requiring total commitment to Jesus and his way of life.

Matthew the Tax Collector

In Matthew's gospel, three of the twelve disciples receive special attention. Why does Matthew dwell on them in particular, and what can their stories tell us about discipleship?

The story of Matthew the tax collector's call is very short. The whole story has only one verse (9:9), but it is significant because of the name "Matthew." Careful readers will notice that Mark 2:14 and Luke 5:27 report the same story, but give a different name to the disciple—"Levi, son of Alphaeus." To explain this conspicuous discrepancy concerning an important apostle, ancient tradition held that the author of the first gospel must have been the disciple Matthew; otherwise, he would have been less confident about his source over against the gospel of Mark, from which Luke adopts the story and the name.

Regarding the calling of Matthew, three important points are worth noting. First is the note of self-possessed authority—Jesus simply says, "Follow me," and without hesitation Matthew obeys and follows him. Second is the fact that Matthew is a tax collector in Capernaum, holding a lucrative job in a prosperous city that is located on the intersection of two major highways. And yet when Jesus calls him, Matthew quickly abandons his position as if nothing in the world could hold him back. It is also important to note the story that follows Matthew's call, a controversy story in which the Pharisees complain against Jesus for dining with tax collectors and sinners. In their minds, Jesus has violated the law of purity when he associates with sinners, especially tax collectors like Matthew who served the Roman Empire to exploit and defraud the Jews. Hearing their charge, Jesus quotes a proverb to defend himself—"Those who are well have no need of a physician, but those who are sick"—and declares, "For I have come to call not the righteous but sinners" (9:12, 13). In this context, Matthew the disciple becomes the best evidence of Jesus' unusual mission to save sinners and the best proof of his power to change lives. Even a tax collector can be transformed.

My third point is that the story of Matthew's call also serves as polemic against the rabbis in late first century. Matthew's gospel reports Jesus' words to the Pharisees: "Go and learn what this means: 'I desire mercy, not sacrifice'" (9:13a). To recruit Matthew the tax collector to be his disciple, Jesus is showing the world how God loves mercy and is ready to welcome back any sinner who repents. Through this calling story we see the generous love of God that subverts our human tendency to classify and criticize others, as well as Jesus' kindness as he includes an unworthy sinner into his circle of friends. Last but not least is the leap of faith the tax collector must take when Jesus calls him, a response that completely changes his life.

Simon Peter

Peter and his brother Andrew are fishermen from Bethsaida living in Capernaum, where Jesus cured his mother-in-law of fever. He is one of Jesus' earliest disciples, following him from Galilee to Jerusalem. After Jesus' death, he becomes a major leader of the church in

Jerusalem, traveling through Judea, Samaria, Caesarea, and Antioch to preach and heal; according to legend he was martyred in Rome under Nero. Among the twelve, Peter is the most fascinating disciple—outspoken, impulsive, always eager to raise the difficult questions. He is also full of contradictions, confessing Jesus to be the Messiah, but refusing to accept his suffering. He usually acts before he thinks, which is why he almost drowns while trying to walk to Jesus across the water and cuts off a high priest's servant's ear trying to defend Jesus. He has the courage to enter the high priest's courtyard to see Jesus on trial, but he also denies Jesus three times. He boasts about never deserting Jesus, but runs into hiding when Jesus is crucified. Yet he preaches Jesus' resurrection with boldness, performs miracles with authority, and leads the church in missions to the Jews, the Samaritans, and the Gentiles. In him both God's grace and human fragility are abundantly evident.

In Matthew's gospel, Peter is a leader among the disciples, the "rock" of faith on which Jesus' church is founded. Furthermore, his stature as leader of the disciples increases as the narrative unfolds, beginning with his attempt to walk on water in Matthew 14. In this story the disciples are crossing the lake in a boat battered by the waves. Early in the morning, they are terrified by the unexpected arrival of Jesus, mistaking him for a ghost. Peter jumps over the boat to walk on water toward Jesus. He is remarkably brave, but begins to sink and has to be rescued; Jesus chides him for his "little faith" but calms the sea. It is at this point that the disciples in the boat worship Jesus, recognizing him as the Son of God. This is a miracle story that illustrates Jesus' divine power to command nature; it is also a paradigm story about the importance of faith because of the character of Peter. To Matthew's first readers, it would have been particularly relevant. If the boat battered by the waves at night symbolizes the church suffering hostility from the Roman Empire and the synagogue, Peter's prayer ("Lord, save me!") teaches them how to overcome danger by faith.

If the boat battered by the waves at night symbolizes the church suffering hostility from the Roman Empire and the synagogue, Peter's prayer ("Lord, save me!") teaches them how to overcome danger by faith.

In chapter 16 we have what is known as the confession of Peter. Traveling through the district of Caesarea Philippi, on the way to Jerusalem, Jesus asks his disciples an essential question about his identity:

> "Who do people say that the Son of Man is?" And they said, "Some say John the Baptist, but others Elijah, and still others Jeremiah or one of the prophets." He said to them, "But who do you say that I am?" Simon Peter answered, "You are the Messiah, the Son of the living God." (16:13–16)

Delighted with his answer, Jesus calls Peter's words a direct revelation from God his Father in heaven. Then, in front of all disciples, Jesus declares, "I tell you, you are Peter, and on this rock I will build my church, and the gates of Hades will not prevail against it" (16:18). There have been many debates on what the "rock" of the church means—Peter himself, or his confession of faith—but there is no doubt that Peter is granted a distinguished status among the twelve.

He is also given the keys to the kingdom of heaven and the authority to "bind and loose." To bind and loose can refer to the power of judicial decisions, and it is also a metaphor for the way in which the rabbis interpreted the scriptures and decided on legal rulings. Peter's judgment, Jesus says, will be honored in heaven. Some interpreters have taken the symbol of the keys and the authority to bind and loose to mean that Peter was appointed gatekeeper for the kingdom of heaven, with the authority to admit and expel people from the church. Others have understood this verse to say that Peter has been assigned to be the church's "chief rabbi" whose responsibility is to unlock the mystery of the kingdom of heaven and explain the meaning of divine revelation to all people on earth. It is noteworthy that the metaphor of "bind and loose" is also used in Jesus' discourse on church leadership and discipline, where it is clearly referring to the judicial authority given to the whole church to expel unrepentant sinners after a due process (18:18). If the judicial authority resides in the whole church, however, it makes better sense to see Peter's authority to bind and loose as the authority to explain Jesus' commandments and form the baptized into faithful disciples. For Matthew, the ultimate mission of the church is to make disciples of Jesus who can obey his commandments. Peter has followed Jesus from Galilee to Jerusalem and has received revelation from God to understand Jesus' identity, so Matthew may mean that Jesus has passed the mantle of his teaching authority to Peter.

Peter is also one of three witnesses to Jesus' transfiguration on a high mountain. Overhearing Jesus' conversation with Moses and Elijah, in his excitement Peter offers to build three tents as shelters so that they may continue their conversations. Then he hears a voice from heaven calling Jesus the beloved Son of God and commanding him to listen to Jesus. This epiphany story shows that Peter is blessed with direct revelation from God and is given the privilege to see Jesus' glory, so he understands Jesus' divine identity and teachings. His earlier confession of faith is now validated on the mountain of the transfiguration.

Why is Peter featured so prominently in Matthew's gospel? In Matthew's view, Peter was undoubtedly the most prominent disciple of the twelve and the leading apostle of the church. The fact that he visited Antioch at the time of Barnabas and Paul (Gal. 2:11–14) suggests that Matthew may have considered him one of the patron saints of his church and wanted his readers to learn from him lessons in discipleship. Peter is uneducated, a working man, but he follows Jesus with enthusiasm and tenacity. He fails sometimes to understand Jesus' teaching or trust in his power, but even more than the other disciples he shows eagerness to learn and the honesty to believe. Although a man of many flaws, God grants him the authority to guide and lead the church. In Peter's stories, we see how Jesus calls, nurtures, and trains him to become a disciple maker. He provides a good example of how a believer may respond to God's grace and Jesus' teaching, and grow into a disciple who serves as a faithful and competent leader of the church.

The most controversial issue about Peter is the nature of his authority. In Matthew's gospel he is the major guardian of the church's doctrine, yet how has the church interpreted Jesus' saying about Peter's authority?

The most controversial issue about Peter is the nature of his authority. In Matthew's gospel he is the major guardian of the church's doctrine with regard to Jesus' identity and teaching. Yet how has the church interpreted Jesus' saying about Peter's authority? We have already seen that after he confesses Jesus to be the Messiah and the Son of God, Jesus responds, "I tell you, you are Peter, and on this rock I will build my church, and the gates of Hades will not prevail against it" (16:18). Jesus seems to speak clearly, but in the history of interpretation, this text is anything but clear. Depending on how one defines the narrative context for this text, there are three ways to see what "this rock" may refer to: the one who confesses (Peter himself), the confession (the revelation regarding Jesus), and the confessed (Jesus as the cornerstone that the builders reject).

Roman Catholic tradition sees Peter himself as the rock of the church, and it does so for good exegetical reasons. *Petros* means "rock or stone" in Greek, and this play on words supports this interpretation. The fact that Peter was widely honored as premier apostle of the church also endorses this reading. This first interpretation is well received in the Roman Catholic Church because it also confirms the primacy of Peter and thus can be used as biblical evidence to support its claim to papal supremacy.

Protestants, however, have argued that it is Peter's confession of faith in Jesus that is "the rock" of the church. Out of all the disciples, Peter is given the keys of the kingdom of heaven and the authority to bind and loose not because of who he is, but because he represents the church that confesses Jesus as the Messiah and the Son of God. It is a confession by faith because Jesus has not yet been crucified and resurrected; thus Peter's confession does not come from his own understanding, but by God's revelation. As such it is pure grace. Furthermore, this tradition holds that Peter cannot be the rock of the church, because shortly after this Jesus tells him, "Get behind me, Satan!" when he tries to prevent Jesus from going to Jerusalem to suffer. Hence, the narrative context shows that it is not Peter, but his confession of faith that is the rock of the church.

A third interpretation is proposed by Augustine, who believed the rock to be Christ himself. His reason is that Jesus later cites Psalm 118 to compare himself to a "rock" when talking to the chief priests and the elders in Jerusalem: "The stone that the builders rejected has become the cornerstone; this was the Lord's doing, and it is amazing in your eyes?" (21:42). Jesus is the "rejected stone" to his opponents, but God has made him the "cornerstone" of the church. By looking into the narrative context of the whole gospel, Augustine found that Jesus identified himself as the rock. His exegesis is sounder than that of the first two interpretations because his reading has a good theological argument. Peter can be a premier apostle for the church, but no mere human being can be the foundation of the church. Peter's confession is the basic tenet of faith for the church, but even the best doctrine needs to be reinterpreted for new times. Jesus Christ is the personal revelation of God's love, which never changes; he alone is the rock of the church, the one whom Peter follows and the one to whom Peter confesses. By belonging to Jesus, Peter is given the name "rock" to recognize his affinity with Jesus.

Judas Iscariot

If Simon Peter is portrayed as a representative of the disciples, Judas Iscariot is the antitype. We have no story of Judas' call, but quite a few about his betrayal of Jesus for thirty pieces of silver, followed by his terrible death. Even though he followed Jesus for a long time, the love of money turned Judas into a betrayer. According to Matthew, Judas' plan of betrayal begins when Jesus is dining in the house of Simon the leper in Bethany. When a woman anoints his head with expensive ointment, some of the disciples are angry at her for wasting a luxury ointment that could be sold instead for a large sum of money to help the poor. But Jesus defends her loving gesture, saying that she is preparing him "for burial." The poor, he reminds them, will always be with them but they will not have him for long. The woman is doing a good service to him, so wherever the gospel is proclaimed, "what she has done will be told in remembrance of her" (26:13).

"Then" (*tote* in Greek) Judas goes to the chief priests and asks how much they will give him in exchange for the capture of Jesus, and right away they pay him thirty pieces of silver. This temporal conjunction suggests that something that happened in Bethany, or what Jesus says about the woman anointing him, is the tipping point for Judas. Could it be that Judas feels disillusioned about Jesus, who seems to be wholly focused on his impending death in Jerusalem? That is not the same Messiah he has followed with high hopes. Or could it be because Jesus seems to dismiss the great need of the poor in favor of a woman who is paying him homage? That is not the same Jesus he has admired and given up everything to serve. Or could it even be that the costly price of the alabaster jar of ointment lures

Judas to love money more than Jesus? Even though Jesus admits to be the Messiah and the Son of God, he has been talking about suffering and death all the way to Jerusalem. What is the point of following him any longer? Judas may have lost the confidence in Jesus and the enthusiasm for the kingdom of heaven. And if he is leaving Jesus, then money is what he needs.

Jesus knows that Judas has wavered in his loyalty, so at the last supper Jesus tells his disciples in great distress that one of them will betray him:

> "The one who has dipped his hand into the bowl with me will betray me. The Son of Man goes as it is written of him, but woe to that one by whom the Son of Man is betrayed! It would have been better for that one not to have been born." (26:23–24)

Jesus is heartbroken that he will be betrayed by one of the twelve disciples he has chosen, loved, and taught for so long. He knows that what has been prophesied in Scripture will surely happen to him. He has no qualm about his suffering and he will not dodge it, but he is so disappointed that he curses the betrayer. Like other stunned disciples, Judas asks Jesus whether he is the one, and Jesus acknowledges it is so, but neither the curse nor the acknowledgment makes Judas change his mind. Undeterred, he goes to the chief priests and the elders and brings a large crowd with swords and clubs to arrest Jesus. In the garden of Gethsemane, he kisses Jesus to tell the crowd whom they are to arrest; a sign of intimacy becomes a sign of betrayal.

Judas' story ends with his suicide. Seeing Jesus unjustly condemned, Judas suddenly comes to senses. Feeling deep remorse for what he has done, he tries to return the silver to the chief priests and the elders, telling them, "I have sinned by betraying innocent blood!" (27:4). It is noteworthy that the Greek verb used for Judas' state of mind is *metamelomai,* meaning "regret or remorse" for a wrong action. It is a different verb from *metanoeō,* which means "repent" in the religious sense. For example, when John the Baptist preaches, "Repent, for the kingdom of heaven has come near," he uses the verb *metanoeō.* The word is also used of the Galilean cities that reject Jesus and refuse to "repent." In view of the difference between the two verbs, Matthew may be suggesting that Judas' remorse is not quite the same as repentance; no matter how deep his regret, he has no opportunity to change what he has done. Devastated, Judas goes out to hang himself and his blood money is used to buy a potter's field to bury foreigners—"the field of blood"—which may fulfill an ancient prophesy by Jeremiah or Isaiah. Judas' story shows that we cannot always foresee the terrible consequences of our

> *Matthew may be suggesting that Judas' remorse is not quite the same as repentance; no matter how deep his regret, he has no opportunity to change what he has done.*

decisions; it can be too late for remorse. In a way, Judas' tragic fall becomes a stark contrast to Peter's rise to apostleship.

In a fourth-century Coptic manuscript discovered recently in Egypt, the *Gospel of Judas,* he is claimed to be the truest disciple of the twelve. Contrary to the traditional view, Judas is portrayed as fully understanding Jesus' message and God's plan. In handing Jesus over to the authorities for trial, therefore, the *Gospel of Judas* argues that he is doing Jesus' bidding, with full awareness of the curse he will bring upon himself and its consequences. When Jesus says at the last supper that his betrayer will be cursed, Judas understands it as a warning and yet is willing to take on the burden out of his wish to help Jesus accomplish his task to die a redemptive death. One of the key verses in the *Gospel of Judas* is a saying by Jesus: "You will sacrifice the man that clothes me." This saying is a "secret revelation" that was given to Judas and meant to exonerate his betrayal of Jesus for money, turning his betrayal into a holy act of sacrifice.

This revisionist view of Judas is highly imaginative and very audacious indeed from the perspective of the traditional Christian belief. It is understandable, however, when placed in the context of the ecclesial and theological debates of late antiquity because it reflects a fierce battle over apostolic authority between the orthodox church and the Gnostics during the third and fourth centuries. The orthodox church honored Peter as the leading apostle who was given the authority to teach and safeguard the Jesus tradition, but the Gnostics considered Judas the truest disciple because he had been given the secret revelation by the risen Christ. The *Gospel of Judas* was written by a dissenting group almost two hundred years later than Matthew, and was clearly intended to contradict and gainsay the orthodox church. It is important historically because it preserves the sectarian

THE GOSPEL OF MATTHEW

beliefs of a Gnostic group of that period, and also informs us of their passionate debates with the traditional church. This gospel is theologically questionable, however, because it appeals to secret revelations privy only to its own community, while the four canonical gospels of the New Testament at least share some common traditions from much earlier sources.

We may wonder whether or not Judas can claim some credit for the role he plays in Jesus' death; after all, it is a death that turns out to be an essential part of God's plan of salvation. This thesis is problematic for several reasons. First, Judas is not essential to Jesus' death or to God's plan of salvation; without his agency, the chief priests and the elders would have still seized and condemned Jesus. Second, it is God who shines light into darkness and brings good out of evil to make Jesus' death on the cross a triumphant act of redemption. For that reason, it would defy credibility to think that Judas, the chief priest, the elders, Pilate, or the Roman soldiers deserve any credit. Third, these human agents have become the devil's instrument in their attempt to get rid of Jesus. For his part, Judas is guilty of greed and betrayal. He might not have intended to get Jesus killed, but his greed and betrayal make him an accomplice to a murder. In Matthew's view, Judas is clearly guilty and his suicide indicates that he has condemned himself for his sins.

> We may wonder whether or not Judas can claim some credit for the role he plays in Jesus' death; after all, it is a death that turns out to be an essential part of God's plan of salvation.

We have seen that Matthew's gospel shows three concentric circles of people surrounding Jesus. At the outermost ring are the crowds who hear and observe Jesus from a distance. They are astounded by Jesus' teaching and miracles, excited by his entry to Jerusalem, and surprised by his silence at his trial. In general, they are curious about who Jesus is. In the middle circle are the friends and followers who encounter Jesus as a savior and confess him as their Lord. They exhibit impressive qualities of love, humility, and faith. They may not have been chosen to accompany Jesus on his ministry, but they are the ones who share their experiences of him with families and friends in their hometowns, and testify to his compassion and power through their transformed lives. Closest of all is the inner circle of the twelve disciples, who are individually chosen and called to follow Jesus so that they may learn from him about the kingdom of heaven and make disciples of all nations for Jesus. The Great Commission indicates that in the final analysis, every person is invited to step out of the observing crowds to follow Jesus and answer his call to become his disciple. All believers should become disciples like the first twelve.

What can we learn from Matthew's stories about Jesus' followers and disciples? If we read them as a window opening onto the divine world, we see some remarkable traits of Jesus. He is happy to enter a Roman centurion's house to heal his servant. He is willing to change his mind and liberate the Canaanite woman's daughter from demons. He is ready to heal the two blind men. He invites Matthew the tax collector to be his disciple. He encourages Peter to ask questions, to try him, and to grow in leadership. He allows Judas to make his choice even though it breaks his heart and gets him arrested and killed. As a teacher, Jesus is compassionate, wise, and patient.

The Great Commission indicates that in the final analysis, every person is invited to step out of the observing crowds to follow Jesus and answer his call to become his disciple.

If we look at those stories as if in a mirror, we also see in those characters reflections of our own lives. The Roman centurion's faith, the Canaanite woman's persistence, the two blind men's determination, Matthew's readiness, Peter's passion, and Judas' mistake let us see with some clarity who we are and what we can be. They serve as excellent models for discipleship. In Peter and Judas, we also see how flawed the disciples can be. It gives us comfort to know, however, that even in our imperfection, Jesus loves us. He will give us time to grow and will lend us support if we ask. Discipleship is both call and gift.

NOTES

1. Ulrich Luz, "The Disciples in the Gospel according to Matthew," in *Studies in Matthew* (Grand Rapids: Eerdmans, 2005), 131–37.
2. Dietrich Bonhoeffer, *The Cost of Discipleship* (New York: Simon & Schuster, 1995), 89–90.
3. Martin Hengel, *The Charismatic Leader and His Followers* (New York: Crossroad, 1981).

CHAPTER SIX

The Church of Jesus

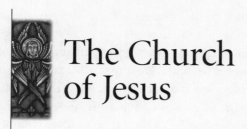

There are different ways to characterize American culture in relation to religion at the present time. Based on his examination of the recent history of legal cases concerning religious freedom as a constitutional right and several controversies over Christian practices, Stephen Carter describes the American culture as a "culture of disbelief" in which religious devotions are being trivialized by law and politics. With the culture wars raging on between the liberal left and the religious right, many public debates in political realm and on social issues have intensified the rhetoric. In our society, the voices of Judaism, Islam, and atheism further amplify the cacophony. American culture today may be aptly labeled as secularizing, postmodern, and diversifying. Different traditions and values certainly enrich our common life, and competition may encourage greater creativity. The challenge, however, is to maintain an open discourse and productive exchange among people of varying beliefs and convictions on social issues and public affairs; it is essential that every proposal is made in good faith and every voice heard with genuine respect. At the conference table, everyone should be welcome as an equal partner of conversation. In order to seek common ground and achieve common goals in a pluralistic society, sometimes it is necessary to suspend one's own agenda and overlook the disagreements with others. In order to get beyond stereotypes and reach a deeper structural understanding of each other's belief system, however, all must articulate their fundamental convictions and share their unique traditions with one another. Everyone should be willing to listen and learn from each other.

It is imperative that the church, like any other religious group and civil association, not be shy in voicing its views and values on important issues in the public square. The church may still command some historical influence, but it should make its perspectives and positions known to the society by words of persuasion and deeds of charity, not by tradition or coercion. If the church believes it is God's people and its mission is to bear witness to God's love in Christ, it should not be absent from public conversations. In order to fulfill its mission to share God's love in the world, however, all members of the church need to know who they are and how to behave beyond the walls of the church. The questions concerning the church's distinctive character and social role are particularly urgent today, because members in all denominations are steadily dwindling and their impact on public life is increasingly sidelined. Do we still need the church? What should the church be like? What are the church's purposes?

In the face of these questions, what insights does Matthew's gospel have to offer? New Testament writings have much to say about the church in terms of its origin and missions (the Acts of the Apostles), its nature (Ephesians, Colossians), its structure (the pastoral epistles), and its theological debates and pastoral concerns (Paul's epistles). Unlike those books, Matthew's gospel is a story about Jesus, set in a time before the church came into existence. Matthew may have some experiences and insights about the nature and character of the church, but his gospel does not directly discuss those issues. However, his intended readers are members of a faith community, and he tells the story of Jesus with a view to addressing the challenges from inside and outside of that community. His understanding of that particular com-

Unlike the book of Acts and Paul's epistles, Matthew's gospel is a story about Jesus, set in a time before the church came into existence.

munity in its own historical setting may still be valuable and useful for us today. So we will begin with what we can find about his church in Antioch in late first century and then discuss what particular traits he thinks are most essential for the church to have and how they might be relevant to the challenges and tasks of our church today.

Matthew's Church

Even though his story of Jesus is set in a time before the birth of the church at Pentecost, it is significant that Matthew uses the term "church" three times in his narrative and he is the only evangelist to do so. The word appears for the first time in 16:18 where Jesus says to Peter, "On this rock I will build my church," after Peter confesses Jesus to be the Messiah and the Son of God. The word appears again in 18:17 (twice) in the context of Jesus' discourse on church discipline with regard to offenders who sin against fellow church members and refuse to repent. After repeated attempts to persuade them to reconcile, the "church" has the authority by consensus to expel such offenders.

In both contexts, the word "church" is used to refer to an organized community of people who follow Jesus. The anachronistic projection of the term back to a historical account suggests that, while reporting Jesus' sayings, Matthew is thinking of the church that was born after the Pentecost, and perhaps his own community of Jewish Christians. The Greek word for "church" is *ekklēsia*, from "called forth," which means the assembly of free citizens who are called forth to discuss and decide on political and national matters. A few scholars have suggested that Matthew uses the word not in the technical sense of the later institutionalized church, but in the common sense of the assembly of Jesus' followers. However, *ekklēsia* is also the word used in the Septuagint to translate the Hebrew word *qahal,* the assembly of God's people. Since Matthew has cited several scriptures from the Septuagint, it is most probably that he has the assembly of God's people in mind when he uses this word. What Jesus says about his followers, then, has to do with his church as a community of God's people, who are called out of all nations to follow Jesus.

Reading Matthew's gospel for sociological clues, moreover, we can see that his church has established itself as a religious community with a clear sense of identity and purposes, with an institutional structure and routine activities as a social group. First of all, they now call their group a "church," distinguished from the "synagogue" from which many of their members came. They may have also used the name *ekklēsia* from the scriptures to imply that they, rather than the people in the synagogue, are the authentic biblical people of God, the true and faithful remnant.

In the second place, Matthew's church has produced a gospel to serve as the foundational document of their community, which tells the story of Jesus, their Lord, in whom they believe and to whom they pledge their allegiance. Jesus' commandments are their laws, his deeds their examples. Jesus' story also functions as the story of origin for their church, because they follow Jesus as his disciples. They also have a creed of faith, confessing Jesus to be the Messiah and the Son of God, which is believed to be a divine revelation passed down from Peter the Apostle. Jesus is not simply a prophet who can work miracles or a teacher of the ordinary kind, but the anointed one of God who comes to save his people from sins, and the Son of God with divine authority.

This community uses liturgies for its common worship, including the Lord's Prayer, the eucharistic meal, and baptism in the name of the Father, Son, and Spirit. Evidently, they have rituals for initiation, prayer, and renewal. They know how to recruit, admit, and consolidate their membership to create a closely knit community. To maintain this community, a variety of leaders perform different functions to safeguard their beliefs and maintain their boundaries—apostles, prophets, teachers, and scribes. There seems to be occasional friction among the leaders, so some sayings of Jesus are brought to bear on internal problems, and they have developed a procedure to promote reconciliation and, when necessary, to discipline offenders who breach the bond of love in the community. Last but not least, they have a well-defined goal of mission to preach the gospel to all nations and turn them into disciples of Jesus. It is a goal set by Jesus Christ their Lord, so it is regarded as the most important task of their church. This mission goal requires his church to become a serious school for learning to obey Jesus'

To maintain this community, a variety of leaders perform different functions to safeguard their beliefs and maintain their boundaries—apostles, prophets, teachers, and scribes.

commandments, and an open community welcoming all peoples to join. By all indications, Matthew is writing for an established church that is organized and institutionalized.

As a social group, Matthew's church is beset by conflict. There are internal disagreements rising from its multiethnic and multicultural membership, and among its leaders vying for authority and honor. There are external challenges from the rabbis and the synagogues who question the church's legitimacy, faith, and practices, along with pressures from the Roman authorities who keep a tight lid on the church in the name of the peace and order of the empire. As a minority group trying to survive in a hostile environment and prove its validity, it is very difficult for Matthew's church to hold its beliefs, to live its way of life, and to share its vision with others.

The Nature and Character of the Church

Like Matthew's church, the church today faces enormous challenges. It may still have historical influence in some parts of the country, but a growing population looks at it with indifference, if not with hostility. Now, in everything that it does or says, the church has to demonstrate its legitimacy and worth to the society. If the church still believes it is God's people called forth to serve as the salt of the earth and the light of the world, what kind of community should it be? If it still believes it should be an agent of change to help bring justice and peace to all—the rich and the poor, the powerful and the oppressed—what kind of character should it exhibit? If it does not want to be shoveled aside by the society, what should it do as a community of faith each and every day? Matthew's gospel has four things to say about the nature and character of the church that might help us to address some of these questions.

The Church as a Community of Faith

First, the church is a community of faith. Matthew uses the word "church" for the first time in Caesarea Philippi, when Jesus questions his disciples as to what people are saying about him. Evidently Jesus' power to work miracles and his authority to teach the law rank him as a respectable prophet in the minds of the public. Then Jesus asks them about their personal opinions: "But who do you say that I am?" and without hesitation, Simon Peter answers: "You are the Messiah, the Son of the living God" (16:16). Jesus replies, "Blessed are you, Simon son of Jonah! For flesh and blood have not revealed this to you, but my Father in heaven" (16:17). Thus Peter is the first disciple to be given the esoteric revelation about Jesus' identity before his crucifixion and resurrection. God must have favored Peter, and his confession is an important revelation for all to hear. At that moment, Jesus says to Peter: "On this rock I will build my church and the gates of Hades will not prevail against it" (16:18). We have already discussed how his words can be interpreted—it is Jesus himself who is the "rock" rejected by the chief priests and the elders but by God's doing has become the cornerstone. Thus his church will be built on him. Here Jesus' church is envisioned in a metaphor of architecture: there are doors, windows, and roofs in a building, but all must be grounded and situated on a solid foundation.

Peter's confession tells us that the church is a community of faith. The object of its faith is Jesus, and the most important content of that faith is who Jesus is—the messianic savior whom the Jewish people have been awaiting and the Son of God who shares the nature, character, and authority with God. In offering his confession to Jesus, Peter represents the church as a community of faith that pays homage and pledge allegiance to Jesus. Right faith in Jesus is directly related to the right understanding of the truth and the right way of life. After he is granted this revelation about Jesus, Peter's task is to explain it to the church so that all believers may understand the mystery of the kingdom of heaven. He is also given the authority to interpret Jesus' teachings for the church so that all believers may know how to conduct their lives worthy of Jesus' name.

It matters what the church believes, and to whom it is devoted; otherwise it is nothing more than an interest group or social club. According to Matthew, there are four symbolic pillars on which the church stands, and the first of these is that Jesus is the Messiah and the Son of God.

It matters what the church believes, and to whom it is devoted; otherwise it is nothing more than an interest group or social club. According to Matthew, there are four symbolic pillars on which the church stands, and the first of these is that Jesus is the Messiah and the Son of God, the anointed one whom God will send to save God's people from their physical and spiritual suffering. For Matthew the root cause of human suffering is sin, so he portrays

Jesus as one born to save his people from sin. Jesus' unfailing compassion and healing powers, his redemptive death and glorious resurrection further testify that he can save his people from sin and death. Jesus is also the Son of God, and to confess him as the Son is to believe that he has a unique status higher than Moses and the prophets and he has an intimate relationship with God. This is why Jesus' teaching about the mystery of the kingdom of heaven and the new way of life is authoritative and trustworthy. He has perfectly shown how we should serve God. To confess Jesus as the Messiah and the Son of God is, in short, to accept him as the most authoritative mediator of God's salvation and revelation.

The second pillar is the belief that God is our Father in heaven. Like other Jews, Jesus believes that the Lord God is the creator of the world, the only true and living God. God alone deserves to be worshipped and God's law obeyed, so it is truly radical for Jesus to claim God as his Father. It is even more radical for him to teach his disciples to call upon God as "our Father who art in heaven." Jesus speaks of God as a loving Father who feeds the birds in the sky and clothes the lilies in the fields and will surely love us even more. God as a loving Father also promises to hear our prayer and gives us better things than we can ask for simply because we are God's children. Moreover, because of the Father's powerful protection and thoughtful provision, we do not need to worry about our daily needs but can try first to fulfill the mandate of God's kingdom and God's righteousness. Jesus also teaches that God the Father is fair and just, before whom all hearts are open and no secret is hidden. God knows our deepest thoughts when we keep fast and give alms, so we should do all good deeds from the heart and not from egotism. Finally, God our Father is perfect, so we are urged to be perfect as God is. One example of God's perfection is inclusive love, which sends the sun to shine on the righteous and the wicked, and allows the rain to fall on the good and the bad. We are thus to imitate God by loving our enemies and praying for our persecutors.

The kingdom of God has come and the world will be transformed. This is the third pillar of the church—its conviction that the kingdom of heaven has arrived just as Jesus announced it, and we must change our lives accordingly. The kingdom of heaven is a metaphor to evoke the vision of the wonderful reign of God, which is characterized by mercy and justice and far better than any political regime or social system in the world. Jesus claims that this new world order has been made available to all; through his healing and teaching he has given us a blueprint of this kingdom. He commands his disciples to pray for its speedy coming and to live into that new reality. When the church, as a social group and a subculture, transforms its way of life to embody this new belief system, it will serve not only as a witness to the reign of God but an effective agent of change to transform the corrupt world order and its political, economic, and cultural structures.

The fourth pillar is this: we are the children of God and the church is the new people. By virtue of believing in God as our Father in heaven, we become God's beloved children as Jesus has always been. This new identity gives us an incentive to shun hypocrisy, vainglory, and other sins, and to live a life worthy of God's name; it also bestows a sense of belonging and solidarity as we serve and change our society. The church becomes the household of God, holy and honorable, whose duty is to reflect the mercy and justice of God our Father. The church is also the new people, who are expected to bear the fruits of the higher righteousness Jesus has commanded. In this world, our life is full of joy but also of sorrow, excitement but also anxiety, hope but also despair. The conviction that God loves us as children gives us the courage and strength we need to be a bold witness, a joyful servant, and an effective agent of change. As the church, then, we can show the world that we are the new people of God, called forth by an inclusive and generous love and committed to serve and refresh the world that God so loves.

The Church as a Community of Love

It also matters how the members of the church live together as a community and how they relate to others outside the church. Matthew's church is a racially mixed and culturally diversified church struggling with ethnic tension, doctrinal disputes, and power struggles. It is a field with wheat and weeds growing side by side, a wedding banquet with good and bad guests, not unlike many of our churches today. To overcome dissensions and conflicts, Matthew puts a special emphasis on Jesus' teaching on leadership and discipline for the church.

In the first half of chapter 18, Jesus puts the burden of responsibility for the community life of the church squarely on the shoulders of its leaders, represented by the disciples. One of their main tasks is to care for all members, especially what Jesus calls "the little ones"—children, the socially downtrodden, and the vulnerable, who can be easily frustrated, led astray, or set back, like the seeds that fall on the path, on rocky ground, and among thorns. These little ones in the church look up to their leaders to learn about the truth and transform their lives, so leaders should pay special attention to their personal lives as well as their instructions in order not to scandalize such members. If they should become stumbling blocks to those little ones, there will be horrible consequences. Jesus warns that if their hands or feet cause them to sin, they may as well cut them off because "it is better for you to enter life maimed or lame than to have two hands or two feet and to be thrown into the eternal fire" (18:8). The church is a community of love; if anyone causes even the least of them to stumble, he or she shall be held liable. Our society has become so polarized that the homeless and the jobless are often shunned or even criminalized. It seems at times that we live in a world in which the fittest survives and the winner takes all, but if we can follow Jesus' commandment to care for each other, especially the little ones among us, the church will become a community of love and a desirable alternative.

One of their main tasks is to care for all members, especially what Jesus calls "the little ones"—children, the socially downtrodden, and the vulnerable, who can be easily frustrated or led astray.

The church is a human association in which personal conflict is inevitable, so Jesus lays out a process for the disciples to solve that problem. If someone is hurt by a fellow member, the injured party is encouraged to speak honestly in private with the offender. If the offender refuses to admit guilt, the injured party can take one or two other members to speak with the offender again as witnesses. The point is to have objective mediators present to reconcile the two parties. If this fails, the case should then be reported to the whole community and, if the offender refuses to admit any fault and make amends, he can be excommunicated (18:17). This mediation process reflects a thoughtful attempt to seek reconciliation before the matter goes to court. Thus individual rights and personal dignity are safeguarded, and several attempts to make peace are required. To uphold justice, Jesus also gives the church the authority of expulsion as the final resort. However, he quickly adds:

> "Again, truly I tell you, if two of you agree on earth about anything you ask, it will be done for you by my Father in heaven. For where two or three are gathered in my name, I am there among them." (18:19–20)

Even though it is necessary for the church to have a process of discipline to deal with internal strife and maintain boundaries, it is in harmony and agreement that their prayers will be answered and it is in unity and concord where Jesus will be present.

In the second half of chapter 18, Peter asks Jesus how often he should forgive a fellow believer who sins against him. As many as seven times? (Seven is a perfect number, so Peter may have meant complete forgiveness.) But Jesus' answer is a surprise—not seven times, but seventy-seven (or seventy times seven) times. In other words, unlimited forgiveness is what Jesus asks of his disciples. There cannot be a stronger emphasis than this on the need of forgiveness in the church. In a community of love, all offenses among the members can be and should be forgiven without limit. But it is not fair to ask the injured party to keep forgiving their offenders, is it? In anticipation of this question, Jesus gives Peter a reason by telling the parable of the unforgiving servant. A slave owes his king ten thousand talents and cannot pay back at the time of reckoning. According to the contract, he himself, his wife, his children, and all his possessions have to be sold off for the payment. When he asks for leniency, the king takes pity on him and decides to give him amnesty, forgiving all his debt and releasing him. Then the servant goes out and runs into a fellow slave who owes him a hundred denarii. Without any pity, he seizes him by the throat and demands an immediate payment even though the fellow slave kneels down and asks for leniency with exactly the same words he says to the king. But he refuses to listen and throws his fellow slave into prison. On hearing this the king is greatly enraged, so he summons him and says: "You wicked slave! I forgave you all that debt because you pleaded with me. Should you not have had mercy on your fellow slave, as I had mercy on you?" (18:32–33). The slave is handed over to be tortured until he can pay his entire debt, and Jesus concludes the parable on a note of warning: "So my heavenly Father will also do to every one of you, if you do not forgive your brother or sister from your heart" (18:35). This parable and Jesus' concluding saying clearly indicate why Christians should forgive one another. They have received God's forgiveness, so they should do likewise; a forgiving spirit is not a merit, but a duty. In our world we tend to feel that we always need to act tough in order to defend our own interest, so Jesus' commandment on unlimited forgiveness feels ridiculous and out of place. But forgiveness is precisely the medicine we need if we want to build loving bonds in the family, enjoy harmony in the society, and make peace in the world. Our faith tells us that God in Christ has forgiven all our sins and faults, and now we need to forgive one another in the church, so that we can show the world what the kingdom of heaven can be like.

In addition to his instructions on loving the innocent and vulnerable, loving those who offend against us, and loving to forgive, Jesus also teaches his disciples how to love God and their neighbors. In reply to a lawyer's question, Jesus declares that the greatest and first commandment is "You shall love the Lord your God with all your heart, and with all your soul, and with all your mind" (22:37). But what does it mean to love God with our total being and total strength? As indicated in the Lord's Prayer, it means glorify God's name, fulfill God's will, and promote God's kingdom. That is to say, give priority to God in our thoughts, words, and deeds. Jesus does not simply teach about loving God; he has practiced what he preaches and exemplified his complete love for God in his life and death. The temptation story, for instance, shows how he loves God's words more than his physical needs, how he refuses to put God to the test, and how he worships God alone. In his prayer in the garden of Gethsemane, Jesus shows how honestly he wrestles with God about his impending death and how willingly he submits himself to God's will to die on the cross. It is not always easy—God may send us to Nineveh to preach bad news or to Jerusalem to suffer with Jesus,

In addition to his instructions on loving the innocent and vulnerable, loving those who offend against us, and loving to forgive, Jesus also teaches his disciples how to love God and their neighbors.

but it is when we honestly and willingly agree to do God's bidding that we prove our genuine love.

Worshipping in a magnificent cathedral is an act of loving God, as is offering intercessions and seeking God's will in our lives through meditation. But feeding the poor and fighting for justice are also tangible acts of loving God. The second commandment is, "You shall love your neighbor as yourself" (22:39). Out of the instinct for self-preservation and self-fulfillment, we tend to love ourselves and put our own needs first; our needs often clash with those of others. In concrete terms, loving the neighbor means to empathize with our neighbors in their sufferings and do our best to help as if our own lives depended on it. Most churches support local, national, and international programs to feed the hungry and shelter the homeless, to provide medical assistance to those who cannot afford it, and to rescue and release the victims of disasters and wars. It is what the church as a community of love should do.

The church is further commanded to enlarge its circle of love to include strangers. In the parable of the sheep and the goats, the king says to those who have fed the hungry, welcomed the strangers, and visited the prisoners: "Truly I tell you, just as you did it to one of the least of these of my brothers and sisters, you did it to me" (25:40). Many scholars have argued that "the least of my brothers and sisters" refers to Jesus' disciples and to Christian missionaries who travel from place to place and risk their lives to preach Jesus' gospel. Those who accept them and treat them with hospitality will be commended as the righteous and be rewarded in the final judgment. This interpretation is exegetically sound for the specific life setting of Matthew's first readers. The story therefore functions at the first level as a story of comfort to encourage missionaries of the gospel.

Nevertheless, this parable has two further theological points beyond that historical context. First, Jesus identifies himself with "the least" who suffer in the world. Whether they suffer for the sake of the gospel or for other reasons, Jesus does not overlook them because they are his brothers and sisters. This is one of the most radical insights we have into the love of Christ. Second, Hebrew scriptures have much to say about providing hospitality to travelers and strangers. Abraham welcomes three strangers who turn out to be the angels of the Lord, coming to prophesy the birth of Isaac. People of Israel are commanded to support the strangers and aliens among them because their forebears were once strangers in the land of Egypt. Jesus' parable teaches the same lesson by emphasizing that the church should provide hospitality in generous love to all kinds of strangers, especially those who have been reduced to almost nothing.

But the most challenging aspect of the church as a community of love is Jesus' commandment to love our enemies. We have often heard that it is human to take revenge, and divine to forgive. It is hard enough to forgive those who hurt us, but Jesus wants us to take one more step in the case of our enemies. Is it possible? Because it is so difficult, Jesus teaches us to pray for God's help. If we leave our vengeance to God, we will not be consumed by rage; the cycle of violence is broken and anger has a chance to subside. At the same time, love has the spiritual power to change even our enemies; Jesus exemplified this by dying on the cross for us while we were sinners and enemies of God. The world is in desperate need of the love that can overcome hatred, bring reconciliation, and sustain peace. The most urgent task of the church is thus to embody a community of love to show the world how to create a better future for all.

> It is hard enough to forgive those who hurt us, but Jesus wants us to take one more step in the case of our enemies. Is it possible?

The Church as a Community of Hope

Christians believe that the kingdom of God has arrived with Jesus, but the reign of God will not be fully implemented until Jesus returns to the world as the Son of Man. The "last day" is the time of final judgment to sort out wheat from weeds, sheep from goats, and the righteous from the wicked. It is also the time for renewal for the whole creation, when the children of God will receive eternal life and the twelve disciples will sit on the thrones of judgment with the Son of Man. So the church is a community of hope, knowing that God is in charge even when evil forces seem to rule the world. The church is a community that prays for Jesus to return soon and to get ready for that day of renewal.

In Matthew's church there seemed to be a crisis of faith about this hope. Some of its members may have felt that they suffered persecution for the sake of Jesus but have waited for God's justice too long, so they began to suspect Jesus would never return. If there is no final justice, what was the point of risking their lives to do God's work or disenfranchising themselves to obey Jesus' commandments? Why not go along with the spirit of the time? To reassure his readers, Matthew records Jesus' speech about the signs of the last judgment and includes several parables about final judgment in Jesus' last discourse. When he returns to judge the world, Jesus will be looking for the faithful and wise leaders of the church. Some of them will be praised for their loyalty and awarded with eternal joy, but others will disappoint him. One servant, thinking his master is delayed, beats his fellow servants and indulges himself in eating and drinking. Five bridesmaids do not prepare ahead of time, so when the bridegroom is delayed they are shut out of the wedding banquet. The servant entrusted with one talent does nothing with it, not even banking it to gain some interests, so he is condemned as wicked and lazy.

Today we may think that the whole idea of the final judgment is the way ancient people projected their unexplained fear and hope into the future, when God would sort everything out for them. Nevertheless, it is an integral part of Old Testament prophecy and Jesus' teaching on the coming of the Son of Man. We confess that "he will come again to judge the living and the dead" in the Apostles' Creed. The whole story of God's revelation and Jesus' redemption rests on that eschatological event. Besides, how we look at the end of time has serious consequences for how we think about God's justice and how we live our lives today. So we will be wise to keep it in mind even if we do not fully comprehend it.

There are also those who believe that the merciful God, by default, cannot impose any eternal punishment on people. This is because they see judgment as contradictory to love. In response to this point, however, there is one important question to consider. Even as God selects Israel as the chosen people and loves them, God sends them into exile in order to discipline them when they rebel and refuse to repent. Judgment can be a form of tough love, and love does not necessarily exclude judgment.

How can we make sense of the final judgment? First of all, the final judgment is more about justice than judgment. It answers the question of theodicy—how God dispenses justice. Justice for all requires that the righteous be rewarded and the innocent compensated; the wicked be reproved and the perpetrators punished. The final judgment thus shows how God deals with evil and justice for all people. Second, the final judgment shows that God cares for what people do in their lifetimes. Whatever we do, good or bad, has consequences and we will all be held accountable before God. Hence we learn to take responsibility and own up to our behaviors. Belief in a final judgment might even serve as deterrence against evil deeds and encouragement for repentance.

In the third place, the final judgment also indicates that the world we live in is not all there is to God's plan. It is true that in the present world there are evil people who enjoy prosperity and longevity, and righteous people who suffer and die early. There might not be justice in this world, but the final judgment assures us that there will be justice in God's time. Since Jesus does not disclose many details about the final judgment, we should not allow our curiosity to run wild, nor should we try to wish it away. Even though the final judgment seems to be delayed, at least to some readers in Matthew's church, it is yet another sign of God's unconventional love. God has patiently waited for the people to repent, sending servant after servant and even risking the life of his son to collect dues from the wicked tenants. God is willing to give the people some more time for repentance. This point is very well articulated in the second epistle to Peter:

> But do not ignore this one fact, beloved, that with the Lord one day is like a thousand years, and a thousand years are like one day. The Lord is not slow about his promise, as some think of slowness, but is patient with you, not wanting any to perish, but all to come to repentance. (2 Pet. 3:8–9)

As a community of hope, the church should hold on to the vision of the final judgment, not with fear or vengeance but with great hope— the hope to lead more people to see God's long-suffering love, to reexamine their daily life before God, and to wait for the final justice for all. This is why in the Great Thanksgiving of the eucharist, the whole congregation joins the priest to proclaim the mystery of faith saying: "Christ has died. Christ is risen. Christ will come again."

Church as a Community of Discipleship

If faith, love, and hope are three vital traits of the church envisioned in Matthew's gospel, what is the main task of the church? For an answer, we turn to the Great Commission, the final testament of Jesus to the disciples before he departs from them. Matthew's gospel reaches its climax when the resurrected Jesus meets with his eleven disciples on a mountain in Galilee. The gathering of the disciples before the risen Jesus reminds us of their previous gatherings to hear the Sermon on the Mount, to answer his question about who he is, and to witness his transfiguration. If the gathered disciples represent the church, what they do and what Jesus does on that mountain has important messages for the church today.

If faith, love, and hope are three vital traits of the church in Matthew, what is the main task of the church? For an answer, we turn to the Great Commission, the final testament of Jesus to the disciples.

The first thing the eleven disciples do when they see Jesus is to worship him. Their act suggests that they honor the risen Jesus as God. They believe that God creates life and only God can bring life back from death. The incredible fact that the crucified Jesus has come out of the tomb and is standing alive before their eyes brings them to their knees. Awestricken, they worship him as they do God. The first act of the church, therefore, is to do the same. Previously they knew it was blasphemy to worship anyone but God, but Jesus' resurrection forces them to see him in a radically different light. In time, the church will have to make sense of the relationship between the almighty God who creates the world and the almighty Jesus who comes back to life from death. On that mountain, however, the disciples are completely stunned; they can do nothing else.

This is also what the church experiences. We may not be able to fully comprehend the mystery of God and articulate Jesus' unique relationship with his Father in heaven. Creeds, doctrines, and theological treatises are part of the church's efforts to make sense of the divine presence that enfolds the disciples when the risen Lord Jesus appears to them.

Jesus' resurrection is so out of the ordinary that some disciples find it difficult to believe even though they see him there in person; they harbor doubts in their hearts. Nevertheless, worship is the right response, one that Jesus accepts and blesses. We do not have to wait until we can fully comprehend Jesus to worship him. The facts that he has revealed himself to us and we have experienced his divine presence are reasons enough to worship him. Paradoxically, it is in worship where we are able to receive Jesus' self-revelation. To his worshipping disciples Jesus declares: "All authority in heaven and on earth has been given to me" (28:18). Before his crucifixion, he already has the authority to heal the sick and cast out demons; with the resurrection, he proves he has the authority to conquer death. Now, with his post-Easter appearance, the disciples receive the full revelation that he has been given all authority in the whole universe. Jesus is the almighty Lord that God has appointed to save us from sin and death. To encounter the resurrected Jesus is a privilege, and it is in worship where we will receive his special revelation and recognize his full authority.

The disciples also receive a commission from the risen Jesus. Even though they are not entirely loyal to him before the crucifixion and some do not believe even now, they are given an important mission:

> Go therefore and make disciples of all nations, baptizing them in the name of the Father and of the Son and of the Holy Spirit, and teaching them to obey everything that I have commanded you. (28:19–20)

This commission has two verbs in the imperative voice—go and make disciples. There are also two verbs in participial form—baptizing and teaching—clarifying what they should do to make disciples. The mission Jesus sets for the disciples, and thus for the church, is to go and make disciples of all nations. The disciples know by personal experience what it takes to be Jesus' disciples. On the journey, sometimes they are excited but sometimes weary. Sometimes they understand, but sometimes they don't. Sometimes they are confident; other times they are afraid. They have already done mission works before, to the Jews in Galilee, but there are differences in this new commission. First, they have to travel to foreign places to reach even the Gentiles. Then they have to convince them to accept Jesus as the Messiah and the Son of God and to commit themselves to follow him. Reaching out to unknown people is a challenge. Sharing

Reaching out to unknown people is a challenge. Sharing personal convictions with strangers can be uncomfortable. But these are the first steps of evangelism.

125

personal convictions with strangers can be uncomfortable. But these are the first steps of evangelism.

The disciple-making mission involves two crucial tasks. The first is baptizing people in the name of the Father, and of the Son, and of the Holy Spirit. Before we baptize people, we need to make them believers. So this task requires us to explain who Jesus is and what he has done, and convince them to accept a new belief system with Jesus at the center. Jesus is the Messiah and the Son of God; God is his Father in heaven who graciously accepts us as children; the Holy Spirit has come from God to give him power to heal, to exorcise, and to rise from the dead. As one can imagine, this trinitarian formula is a scandal to Jewish monotheism and Greco-Roman polytheism, but it is a short formula to summarize what Matthew and his church, including Peter and Paul, have experienced about the mystery of God. As a community of discipleship, the church needs to think together and continue to reflect on the creedal formula that tries to capture our religious experiences in the mystery of God. In different times, places, and cultures, the statement of our experiences and beliefs may need to be reformulated, but the church has to be faithful to Jesus Christ, its foundational rock, who has authority in heaven and on earth.

Once a person is convinced of the Christian belief system, baptism is in order. Baptism is a cleansing and initiation ritual. It signalizes the forgiveness of sins and the admission to the church. The first task of making disciples is thus to evangelize, to introduce people to Jesus Christ the Son of God, and to induct them into the church, the community of faith, love, and hope.

The second task of disciple-making is to teach believers to obey everything that Jesus has commanded. When new members join the church, they are like newborns who need nurture and training to grow mature and strong. Discipleship is a journey of faith that requires perseverance. If the disciples who gave up everything to follow Jesus could still be lacking in understanding and weak in faith, how much more so do we need to learn about Jesus' teaching and experience his power? One of the priorities of the church should therefore be to provide educational programs for all its members, so that they may love both Jesus and his teaching. When believers learn to obey Jesus' commandments, they will grow in the knowledge of God's love and their lives will be transformed.

Why is obedience to Jesus' commandments important? Jesus' commandments clarify the meaning of the law and the prophets, and represent God's will by which we will be judged. They guide us to live a new way of life in honor of God and worthy of our status as God's children. By obeying his commandments, we will begin to think and behave like Jesus, and gradually become faithful disciples. If most members are well informed and properly trained in discipleship, the church as a community will be able to display the character of faith, love, and hope to make a positive difference in our society.

In its effort to fulfill this mission, the church will run into barriers and experience setbacks, so it is comforting to know that Jesus promises to be with his disciples until the end of the age.

As a community of discipleship, the church's task is to worship Jesus, to evangelize, and to form the baptized into disciples. In its effort to fulfill this mission, the church will run into barriers and experience setbacks, so it is comforting to know that Jesus promises to be with his disciples until the end of the age. By the power of the risen Jesus who has conquered all, the church will have the courage and wisdom and every chance to accomplish its mission.

Conclusion

What is the nature and character of the church? Matthew has shown us that the church Jesus gathers in his name is first of all a community of faith, built on the conviction that Jesus Christ the Son of God is the foundation of our belief system. Through Jesus' teaching, we also believe in the almighty God as our loving Father in heaven who protects and provides for us and whose kingdom has come in power to transform the world. By divine grace we have become God's children. The church is also a community of love in which the little ones receive special care and the offenders will be forgiven. It is a community in which we learn to love God with all our being and to love neighbors as ourselves. We also learn to love strangers and even our enemies in order to show the world how good God's kingdom can be. The church is also a community of hope. We believe the final judgment reveals God's love for the righteous and God's intention to uphold justice for all. God will hold everyone accountable for what they do in this life. The delay of the final judgment is an evidence of God's long-suffering patience; God wants to give us another chance to repent. So we do not have to be afraid, but can look for its coming as the day of final redemption and great renewal for the world. Finally, the church is a community of discipleship. In worship, we can encounter the resurrected Jesus and receive revelation to experience his divine authority. We are also commissioned to go out and make disciples of all nations by baptizing believers and training the baptized. So the church should engage in evangelism and strengthen education programs to train faithful disciples who understand Jesus' teaching and obey his commandments.

Like the twelve disciples, all Christians are called to walk with Jesus on his journey to Jerusalem. Like the disciples who were so often tempted, we often covet the position of honor in the church and want our opinions accepted. Like the disciples who betrayed, denied, and deserted Jesus when he was arrested, we often shy away from giving personal testimony, participating in social service, or speaking prophetic truth. As a result, the church is sidelined, our voice hushed, and our faith practice trivialized. However, just as the disciples were rejuvenated by meeting with the risen Jesus and empowered to preach the gospel to the whole world, our church can be transformed again to become the city on the hill. All we need to do is to become Jesus' disciples, loving him and obeying him; in so doing, we will be able to build our church as a community of faith, love, and hope.

ACKNOWLEDGMENTS

I would like to thank my students at Virginia Theological Seminary who have participated in my Matthew seminars over the years and contributed to my understanding of this amazing gospel through their searching questions and passionate discussions. I know their preaching and teaching are greatly enriched by wrestling with Matthew—and their churches benefited and blessed for it.

My thanks also go to several Episcopal and Presbyterian churches in the Washington, DC, area where I have had the privilege of teaching Sunday Forums. Their interest in Scripture and their love for the church inspire me to work harder to bring scholarly research to bear on our belief and practice in daily life.

Thanks are also due to Dr. Frederick Schmidt of Perkins School of Theology at Southern Methodist University who first encouraged me to write this book. My deepest gratitude is offered to Cynthia Shattuck, the wonderful editor who patiently and wisely guided me through this book.

Last but not least, I thank God for my dear wife, Su, and my daughter, Janet, whose unlimited love and constant support make my teaching, research, and writing an immensely enjoyable labor. May God bless this book for the good of the church!

Sharon Ely Pearson

The Gospel of Matthew was perhaps the favorite of the early church, offering a carefully crafted account of Jesus' birth, mission, and passion. It is neatly organized for teaching purposes. Following the infancy narrative, baptism, and temptation of Christ, which connects Jesus to the Hebrew Scriptures, Matthew presents many accounts of Jesus' teaching, healings, and missions. The best known, the Sermon on the Mount combines his blessings and teachings that convey his radical message.

Introduction

This study guide is meant to accompany each chapter as a path to go deeper and reflect upon the themes and ideas that the author offers through his overview of Matthew. The questions and reflections will invite you into a conversation about how we connect with the theological themes and motifs that Matthew is sharing with his audience of almost two thousand years ago and how it can have significance to our own understanding of what it means to be a follower of Christ.

The Gospel of Matthew was written between CE 75 and 95. Clues within the book suggest it was written after the Romans destroyed the Jerusalem temple in CE 70. The debate over the authorship of Matthew hinges on the similarities seen in the gospels of Matthew, Mark, and Luke. Matthew has included most of Mark (along with sources from Q and L), though the stories are shortened to leave room for original material, consisting mostly of Jesus' teachings. Its author is an unknown Christian, probably of Jewish background writing for Jewish Christians, possibly of Antioch in Syria. At the time, the

Christian Jewish community was caught in a struggle between their understanding of Jesus as the Messiah and traditional Judaism that was trying to retain its identify after the destruction of the temple.

In Matthew's "good news" you'll not find as much dramatic action as in Mark, or as many spotlights on compassion as you'll read in Luke. But you'll discover the most complete record of what Jesus taught and how his teachings grow out of Old Testament scriptures.

As you begin this study of Matthew, consider the following:

- Why you are engaging in this study of the Gospel of Matthew?
- What have your previous understandings been of this period of time in the early church? Do you go into this study with any preconceived notions? If so, jot them down before reading.
- What do you hope to learn and discern for yourself in this study?
- What was the world like at this period of our world's history? How is it different to today's world? Similar?

Before studying each chapter of this book, portions of Scripture may be suggested to read ahead of time. The passages may not be sequential, as if you are reading the gospel from start to finish, as Yieh explores Matthew from a thematic viewpoint, moving back and forth through the chapters of this gospel. You may also wish to have a map of North and Central Palestine circa CE 30, as well as of the Roman Empire at the time of Paul's journeys. These can be found in the appendix of most study bibles. As you read Matthew, follow Jesus' journeys by looking at the significant places on the map and note what happened at each location.

Chapter One: A New Gospel

The first chapter begins with Dr. Yieh discussing the purpose of eulogies in relationship to the purpose of the gospels in the New Testament. As with any eulogy, we also learn something about the speaker as well as the person sharing their understandings and relationship of the deceased—in this case the Risen Lord. Begin by reflecting on your own relationship with Jesus and the gospels:

- When you hear Jesus' name mentioned, what stories, if any, from childhood to you remember?

- What was the context from which your memory comes? Church? Sunday school? Home? A children's bible? The movies? A sermon?
- What do you believe is the purpose of a eulogy?
- If you were to write a eulogy for Jesus, what would it include? How would you personalize it as someone giving it at His "memorial service"?

Yieh contrasts two viewpoints as to what the gospels are: (a) history and (b) faith. He shares an overview of the types of methods used to read Scripture as well as a comparison of the Synoptic gospels (Matthew, Mark, and Luke).

- What do you believe the gospels are? Do believe along the lines of the historical scholars or those feel faith interpretation must be included?
- What is the purpose of the gospels if they are seen as eulogies of Jesus?
- What is the difference between narrative criticism and redaction criticism of research when studying biblical texts?
- What's the difference between the Synoptic gospels?

The gospel of Matthew has a particular purpose and spin on Jesus' mission and ministry. During your reading of Chapter One, read Galatians 2:11–14 and Acts 13:1–3.

- Describe Mark's portrayal of Jesus and the focus of his gospel. What is the purpose of Matthew writing yet another account of Jesus' life?
- Why does Matthew follow the literary pattern of ancient biography for classical heroes and philosophers in telling the story of Jesus?
- How is ancient biography different than today's biographies?
- How would imitating Jesus (in the early church as well as today) enhance one's spiritual character?
- Why does Matthew accentuate the eschatological warning throughout his gospel?
- Do you agree with Yieh's descriptions of moral and spiritual complacency in the face of nationalism as a focus for Matthew? How might this be similar today?

Chapter Two: Jesus Christ, the Son of God

We begin reading Matthew by setting the stage of who Jesus is. Before beginning, jot down some understandings of who you believe Jesus was (or is) and how you come to these conclusions.

Read Matthew 1:1–2:23

- What is the purpose of listing Jesus' genealogy in Matthew (and its difference from Luke's)?
- Why is Matthew so careful to provide Jesus with impeccable credentials? What would the relationship to David and to Abraham have meant to Matthew's Jewish audience?
- What is important about the birth of Jesus according to Matthew? What seems most significant about the visit of the wise men from the East?
- What does viewing God as active and intentional in human history mean to us today?
- What does it mean to "save his people from their sins"? Who are his people? In what sense do you think of Jesus as Savior?
- As the star directed the magi, what directs you to Jesus? What gifts would you like to offer Jesus? What do they symbolize?

Read Matthew 11:1–15; 16:13–20; 21:1–11, 23–27; 27:32–37, and Psalm 110

- In Matthew 11:3, John the Baptist poses the central question of Matthew's gospel: Is Jesus the Messiah? Restate Jesus' answer in your own words. Why would John have recognized this in an affirmative reply?
- What are the credentials of the Messiah?
- To what does Jesus appeal to convince people of his authenticity?
- In what ways does Peter's confession clarify the issue of Jesus' identity? How would you answer the same question today?
- What kinds of feelings do you have when you contemplate proclaiming Christ publicly?
- Do you agree with Yieh's statement: "Except through Jesus no one can understand God, and only those whom he has chosen will be able to receive revelation"? Why or why not?

After noting that Jesus is the new Moses *(read Exodus 1:1–2:25 and 19:1–20:21 for comparison)*, Yieh describes Jesus' mission as twofold— to reveal God's will and to demonstrate God's love.

- How did Moses exhibit this? Where is the connection with Jesus?
- Why is Jesus' teaching ministry so important to Matthew?
- How does the church today continue to proclaim and teach God's mission as Jesus proclaim it?
- What do you consider the important qualities of a teacher?
- Does a teacher need authority? Why or why not? In today's world, where do teachers get their authority?
- What is the difference between wisdom and knowledge?
- Yieh states that Matthew had three purposes in depicting Jesus as a teacher of God's will who is itinerant, authoritative, wise, and exemplary. Which is most important to you—didactic, polemic, or pastoral?

Chapter Three: The Teachings of Jesus

In this chapter we will focus on the specific teachings of Jesus. His teaching may be summarized in one key idea: "righteousness, which is considered the ticket, task, and goal of God's kingdom." If possible, read the stories in a variety of translations of the Bible, such as the NRSV, The Message, and the Common Bible.

Read Matthew 5

These chapters make up the material known as the Sermon on the Mount, one of the most familiar collections of Jesus' teaching. Though the sermon probably represents fragments of Jesus' teaching that were recalled by oral tradition, the gospel writer has organized them carefully.

- The beatitudes have been interpreted either as divine comfort or spiritual discipline in the history of the church. How do you read and interpret them?
- According to the Sermon on the Mount, what are some of the qualities of discipleship?
- What are the characteristics of the kingdom of heaven?
- To us, the word "heaven" may suggest the next world. To Jews it was more a synonym for God because the Jewish tradition

avoids naming God directly. What does the image of the "king-dom of God" mean to you?

■ How do the values represented in the Beatitudes stand in con-trast to values of past ages in Christianity? In today's conven-tional attitudes and behavior in our society?

■ How could acting on these values—or with these attitudes—effect change in our world?

■ In what ways does your own Christian community provide salt (flavor, zest) and light (direction, clarity) to the larger community? For whom are you "salt" and "light"? Which people are "salt" and "light" for you?

■ Do you agree or disagree with the statement that the Sermon on the Mount "applies only to religious life and church com-munity"?

Read Matthew 6

Jesus' teachings now turn to religious duties and personal piety. Almsgiving, prayer, and fasting are central themes and it is here that we are given "The Lord's Prayer."

■ What does righteousness and piety mean to you? How are they similar or different?

■ Compare Matthew 6:9–13 with Luke 11:1–4. How are they similar? Different?

■ How many times does Jesus tell us not to be anxious? In what ways does anxiety distract us from our true priorities? How does it prevent us from seeing clearly? How does anxiety relate to being overly concerned with laying up "treasures on earth"?

■ Is it possible to make money and love God at the same time?

■ In what ways do we understand fasting, almsgiving, and prayer as necessary "acts of devotion" or "good works" for people today?

Read Matthew 7

Throughout the Sermon on the Mount we note a dual emphasis: righteousness (right relationship with God) that implies a right rela-tionship with other people.

■ Why does Jesus require victims to forfeit their legal right to seek reasonable compensations from their persecutors ("An eye for an eye and a tooth for a tooth")? How difficult is it for you to give up the principal of fair judgment for one of nonjudgment?

- What is your reaction to Martin Luther's view that nobody could fully obey the laws of Christ as set out in the Sermon on the Mount because they function not as a "rule" but as a "mirror," reflecting back to people their sin and deficiency?
- What are some of the "narrow gates" you have chosen in your own life? How did these choices help you to grow in understanding yourself? Other people? God?

Read Matthew 10 and Acts 15

The disciples are to mirror the actions of Jesus described in Matthew Chapters 9 and 10. Like Jesus, they are to work without pay, travel light and trust local hospitality.

- List some of the elements of the task of discipleship discussed in 10:1–15. What personal qualities would equip an individual to undertake this task? Compare your list with Matthew 5:3–11.
- How broadly are the first-century missionary instructions to be applied? What general principals do they suggest for the Church today? For your own life?
- How do we understand inclusivity in the church and mission today?
- Why does Jesus order his disciples to travel light?

Read Matthew 13

Jesus teaches in parables, telling story after story to illustrate the nature of God's kingdom.

- What are the reoccurring images found in these parables?
- What reactions to his teaching does Jesus encounter?
- In what ways is faith itself a help in deepening our understanding of Jesus?
- How is it possible to see and hear the truth without being able to understand it? What things in our lives prevent us from hearing God's word in meaningful ways?

Read Matthew 18:1–35

Jesus' fourth discourse continues his teachings on leadership, humility, and forgiveness.

- Why is the first quality of church leadership humility?
- Why should leaders promote reconciliation at all cost?
- What is the difference between being "childish" and "childlike"? What childlike qualities do you think Jesus has in mind? What are some ways to reclaim these as adults? How can children in our families or communities help us in this endeavor?
- Why do people leave our church communities? What kind of "shepherding" might they need before they are ready to return?
- Why is forgiveness important in the Christian community?

Read Matthew 24–25

In the fifth and final discourse of his gospel, Matthew presents Jesus' teachings about the future. Much of the language is drawn from the Old Testament apocalyptic writings that depict the ultimate destruction of evil and triumph of good.

- What is your response to Jesus' description of "wars and rumors of wars" and all kinds of natural disasters as "birth-pangs"? When there is chaos in our lives, how do we typically respond? How does believing that chaos is the stuff of new beginnings help us to avoid discouragement?
- What does 24:14 suggest we should be doing while in the midst of multiple wickedness, wars, famines, etc.? Who does Jesus expect to preach the gospel throughout the world? How well does today's Church bring Jesus' message of peace to the world?
- What can we learn from all of Jesus' teaching that applies to our own lives?
- Yieh mentions several recent points in history (September 11, the wars in Iraq and Afghanistan, the Nickel Mines tragedy in Pennsylvania) as points to explore God's justice and God's mercy. How should we respond to evildoers and our enemies today?

Chapter Four: Jesus' Opponents

This chapter focuses on the variety of persons and groups who might be perceived as enemies or opponents to Jesus, including the established religious leaders of the day. Read the portions of Matthew and other scripture in which these "characters" show their hostility:

- King Herod the Great (Matthew 2:1–18)
- The Devil (Genesis 3:1–7; Matthew 4:1–11)

- Pharisees and scribes (Matthew 9:9–13; 15:1–20; 16:1–12; 23:1–36
- Chief priests and elders (Matthew 21:23–46)
- Herod Antipas (Matthew 14:1–2 and Luke 26:6–15)

The ongoing dispute between Jesus and the Pharisees accelerates in Matthew 15:1–20. Serious charges are beginning to be made as Jesus and his disciples continue to violate the tradition of the elders (the body of interpretation that developed around the written law and was transmitted orally by rabbis over generations).

- Why are the Pharisees a major source of opposition and hostility to Jesus' teachings, seeing him as a threat to the Temple authorities?
- Yieh paraphrases Jesus' teaching as, "The law is a gift from God to benefit God's people in emergencies. One should not forget human plight while keeping the divine law." Where is this true today?
- Do you believe Jesus "baited" the Pharisees and others in authority by challenging them with his parables, frustration, and anger?
- What does the term "hypocrisy" mean to you?
- How is Matthew apologetic, polemic, and didactic in showing the confrontations between Jesus and the Pharisees?
- Why is Jesus continually being challenged by others in Matthew?
- Why does Jesus refuse to identify where his authority comes from?

Read Matthew 21:28–22:14 and Isaiah 5:1–7

Jesus resumes his teaching by telling three parables about the judgment of Israel.

- Compare the parable of the wicked tenants with the parable of the vineyard in Isaiah. What are the differences? Similarities?
- Which of the three parables in this portion of Matthew speaks to you most clearly about the need to respond to God's call? In what ways can you apply its teachings to your spiritual situation?
- In what ways do we do violence to the servants that God sends to the Church (vv. 34–36)? In what ways do we do violence to Jesus, God's Son (vv. 37–39)?

- In what ways does God's invitation come to people today?
  What is the role of the Church in issuing the invitation?
  In helping those who respond to be "properly dressed"
  for participation?

Read Matthew 26:1–56

The first sixteen verses of Matthew 26 serve as a prologue to the fast-paced narrative that follows. While Jesus calmly states the time and manner of his death, the chief priests and elders nervously plot to bring it about.

- What significance do you see in the setting (house of Simon the leper) for the story of Jesus' anointing? How does it contrast with the setting for the dignitaries' plotting (vv. 3–5)?
- What motives might Judas have as he decides to collaborate with the chief priests? How do you think he feels when he accepts the money? How do you suppose he justifies his action?

Read Matthew 26:57–27:50

Matthew describes Jesus' trial in three parts: (1) a night session of the Sanhedrin in the high priest's palace, (2) a brief morning session, and (3) the trial before Pilate. It results in his crucifixion, with many of his opponents playing a role in his journey to the cross.

- How would members of the Sanhedrin expect one who claims to be the Messiah to behave? What kind of Messiah does Jesus' behavior suggest? What do you think of Jesus' method of dealing with his accusers? Does his silence indicate strength or weakness? Why?
- How do you feel about Pilate's final claim of innocence? How is avoiding participating in a decision similar to or different from actively taking one side or the other? In what way is this an example of "the spirit is willing, but the flesh is weak"?
- Yieh does not believe Matthew's story of the trial can be used to support anti-Semitism, despite what many interpreters in history have believed. How do you understand these passages?
- What three groups mock Jesus while he is dying on the cross? What is the significance of their insults?
- What would have been the outcome if Jesus had come down from the cross? Do you think he was genuinely tempted to

do so? Why or why not? In what ways did his experience in the wilderness with the Devil (tempter) prepare him for this moment?

Chapter Five: Jesus' Followers and Disciples

Yieh begins this chapter with comments about what it means to be a Christian in a culture that is becoming more secular, especially in Europe and North American.

- What does it mean to you to be a Christian?
- What makes a Christian different?
- Why does anyone want to be a Christian?
- How did you become a Christian?
- Yieh says followers of Jesus exhibit three characteristics: love, humility, and faith. Who do you know that possess these? Do you?

"Discipleship is a holy calling that comes with the privilege of relating to Jesus, learning from him, and hearing his promises, but it is a journey of love that leads to the cross."

- What is the definition of discipleship given in the text?
- Why does Matthew use numerology throughout his gospel, especially in choosing twelve disciples?
- Why does one choose to follow Jesus? What is the call that cannot be ignored?
- What is the cost of being a disciple of Jesus?
- Do you agree or disagree? Why?
- How would you define discipleship?

Read Matthew 4:18–20; 14:22–17:27; 19:13–30; 26:30–75

In Matthew's gospel, Simon Peter is a leader among the disciples, the "rock" of faith on which Jesus' church is founded. In 16:18–19 (found only in Matthew) we have the basis for the tradition of apostolic succession, and the Roman Catholic doctrine that Peter was the first of the bishops of Rome, head of the Church universal.

- How would you describe Peter as a follower of Jesus? As a disciple?
- What do you think Peter is thinking as he follows Jesus to the palace? What conflicting emotions might he be experiencing?

- In what ways can you identify with his conflict between his desire to follow Jesus and his instinct for self-preservation? How do you deal with such conflicts?
- Why do you believe the role of Peter is featured so prominently in Matthew's gospel?
- How has the church interpreted Jesus' saying about Peter's authority?
- What can Peter teach us about discipleship?

Read Matthew 26:1–27:9

We have no story of the call of Judas Iscariot, but he plays an important role as the disciple who betrays Jesus.

- What motives might Judas have as he decides to collaborate with the chief priests? How do you think he feels when he accepts the money? How do you suppose he justifies his action?
- Why was Judas disillusioned with Jesus, while the other disciples did not seem to be (at least according to Matthew)?
- Why do we have such different impressions of Peter and Judas, neither of whom behaved very admirably under pressure? What makes the difference? Why did one weep bitterly and the other give in to despair?
- The *Gospel of Judas* portrays a different view of why he betrayed Jesus. What do you feel about this new view of Judas? Why does Yieh disagree?

Read Matthew 28:16–20

The Great Commission invites every person to step out of the observing crowd to follow Jesus and answer his call to become his disciple.

- In what ways do we demonstrate our loyalty to Jesus? In what ways, small or large, do we reject Jesus?
- Do you place yourself as one who hears and observes Jesus from a distance, a follower of Jesus who confesses him as Lord, or one who is chosen and called to follow Jesus by making disciples of others for Jesus?
- What can we learn from Matthew's stories about Jesus' followers and disciples?
- How can discipleship be both a call and a gift? How is it a call? How is it a gift?
- How do you fit into the Great Commission?

Chapter Six: Jesus' Church

Matthew's readers are members of a particular faith community in Antioch in the late first century. There are insights we can learn from this early church as it learned the story of Jesus for our church today.

Read Matthew 16:13–20 and 18:1–14

The word "church" is used to refer to an organized community of people who follow Jesus.

- Who is Jesus to his community of followers (the church)? What is their mission?
- How does this community differ from that of the synagogue of which many of his followers come from?
- What was Matthew's community like? How is this church like (or different) than the denominational churches today?
- Look up "The Church" in An Outline of the Faith (the Catechism) in *The Book of Common Prayer,* p. 854. How is this similar (or different) to the church in Antioch?
- Compare the four symbolic pillars on which the church stands that Yieh describes with The Nicene Creed (BCP p. 358–59) and The Apostles' Creed (BCP p. 96).
- Does the church live out these pillars today? If so, how? If not, why not?
- Who are the littlest in our society today?

Read Matthew 18:15–35; 22:34–40; 25:31–46

The church is a community of love, forgiveness, and reconciliation.

- Why is forgiveness important in the Christian community? How are persistent offenders dealt with in your church community? How difficult do you find it to confront another with wrongdoing? Why do you think Jesus suggests this approach in 18:15–18?
- Rabbis of Jesus' day taught that one should forgive three times for the same offense, but not a fourth time. How does Jesus' reply to Peter's question change this principle? How do you reconcile verse 22 with verse 17? Where do you experience the tension between the need to forgive and the need to discipline?
- What does it mean to forgive "from the heart" (v. 35)? What wisdom do you see in the folk adage "forgive and forget"? What wrongs against you would you like to forget?

- How does the combination of "love of God" and "love of others as of self" provide the link between religious faith and ethics (behavior)?
- What other actions toward "the least of these" would you add to Jesus' list? What other "least" individuals might you add? Why?
- What are some of the tasks that Jesus has entrusted to the church? What sort of work are we to engage in while waiting and watching for the *parousia*?

Read Matthew 28:1–20

- What is the mission of the church today? (Refer to "The Church" BCP p. 855).
- In what ways do you see American society becoming more secularized, postmodern, and diverse in terms of a "culture of disbelief"?
- How should the Church make its perspectives and positions known to the society—by words of persuasion and deeds of charity or tradition and coercion?
- Do we still need the church? What should the church look like? What are the church's purposes?
- Which is more important, the end of history or the process of Christian living?

Concluding thoughts:

- What are the most significant insights you have gleaned from reading the Gospel of Matthew?
- How different are you for having engaged in this study?
- How has your understanding of being a disciple of Jesus changed?
- What does Matthew 28:20 mean to you? How does knowing God is with you impact your life? How do you share this impact with others?

Sharon Ely Pearson *is the Christian Formation Specialist for Church Publishing Incorporated with an MACE from Virginia Theological Seminary.*

CONTINUING THE CONVERSATION: SUGGESTIONS FOR FURTHER READING

Matthew wrote his gospel as a biography to inform the readers of Jesus' remarkable words and deeds so as to transform believers into disciples. The characters, episodes, teachings, and debates are tactically chosen and arranged to demonstrate Jesus' special identity, role, and impact. To understand Matthew's main purposes, it is essential to begin with literary analysis. For an expert guide to its literary design and rhetorical features, see J. D. Kingsbury's two books, *Matthew: Structure, Christology, Kingdom* (Philadelphia: Fortress, 1975) and *Matthew as Story,* 2nd ed. (Philadelphia: Fortress, 1988). For a narrative-critical study of the disciples as literary characters affecting the readers, see R. A. Edwards, *Matthew's Narrative Portraits of Disciples: How the Text-Connoted Reader is Informed* (Harrisburg: Trinity, 1997).

Matthew also wrote his gospel for a mixed church with diverse traditions and ominous crises, so some knowledge of the thorny social-historical contexts of Matthew's community is crucial. For a brief and perceptive history of Matthew's church in Antioch, see Raymond Brown and John Meier, *Antioch and Rome: New Testament Cradles of Catholic Christianity* (London: Geoffrey Chapman, 1983). For an in-depth and balanced discussion of key historical issues regarding its group identity and social relations, see Graham N. Stanton, *A Gospel for a New People: Studies in Matthew* (Louisville: Westminster John Knox, 1993). For a description of the institutionalization of Matthew's community in contention with the rabbis and the synagogues, see D. R. A. Hare, *The Theme of Jewish Persecution of Christians in the Gospel*

According to Matthew (Cambridge: Cambridge University Press, 1967) and J. Andrew Overman, *Matthew's Gospel and Formative Judaism: The Social World of the Matthean Community* (Minneapolis: Fortress, 1990). As an illicit group, Matthew's church also faced political challenges under the Roman rule. To learn more, see John Riches and David C. Sim, eds., *The Gospel of Matthew in Its Roman Imperial Context* (London: T & T Clark, 2005); and Warren Carter, *Matthew and the Margins: A Sociopolitical and Religious Reading* (Maryknoll, NY: Orbis, 2000).

Matthew's gospel contains important theological themes, such as Christology, eschatology, law, and mission, which have formed and shaped the vital traditions of Christian faith and life since its origins. For an excellent collection of essays by major scholars, see Graham N. Stanton, ed., *The Interpretation of Matthew* (Edinburgh: T. & T. Clark, 1995). Another significant collection of essays compares Matthew's theological views with those of other early Christian writers: David Sim and Boris Repschinski, eds., *Matthew and His Christian Contemporaries* (London: T & T Clark, 2008). For Matthew on pastoral-theological questions, see Mark A. Powell, *God with Us: A Pastoral Theology of Matthew's Gospel* (Minneapolis: Fortress, 1995). On Jesus as the supreme teacher of God's will to build up the church, see John Yieh, *One Teacher: Jesus' Teaching Role in Matthew's Gospel Report* (Berlin: de Gruyter, 2004). On Matthew's apocalyptic view undergirding his understanding of Jesus' role and Christian life, see David C. Sim, *Apocalyptic Eschatology in the Gospel of Matthew* (Cambridge: Cambridge University Press, 1996). On Matthew's use of polemic language, see S. McKnight, "A Loyal Critic: Matthew's Polemic with Judaism in Theological Perspective," in *Anti-Semitism and Early Christianity: Issues of Polemic and Faith*, ed. C. A. Evans and D. A. Hagner (Minneapolis: Fortress, 1993), 55–79.

The Sermon on the Mount is the most beloved and controversial section of Matthew's gospel with a long history of interpretations and consequences. A brief introduction to its challenges to our contemporary appropriations can be found in John Yieh, *Making Sense of the Sermon on the Mount* (Cambridge: Grove, 2007). For a comprehensive literary-historical commentary, see Hans Dieter Betz,

The Sermon on the Mount (Minneapolis: Fortress, 1985) and for a brief commentary emphasizing its Jewish heritage, see Dale C. Allison Jr., *The Sermon on the Mount: Inspiring the Moral Imagination* (New York: Crossroad, 1999). Finally, an essay collection that traces the Sermon on the Mount throughout history is Jeffrey Greenman, Timothy Larsen, and Stephen Spencer, eds., *The Sermon on the Mount through the Centuries from the Early Church to John Paul II* (Grand Rapids: Brazos, 2007).

Finally, there are three comprehensive critical commentaries valuable for the study of Matthew in English. W. D. Davies and Dale C. Allison Jr.'s commentary, *A Critical and Exegetical Commentary on The Gospel according to Saint Matthew,* 3 vols. (Edinburgh: T. & T. Clark, 1988, 1991, 1997), provides a treasury of scholarly resources, especially materials from Jewish literature. Robert H. Gundry's *Matthew: A Commentary on His Handbook for a Mixed Church under Persecution,* 2nd ed. (Grand Rapids: Eerdmans, 1994) is a historical-critical exegesis focused on the specific social and historical context of Matthew's church and is cogently argued to expose Matthew's theological contents. Ulrich Luz's three-volume commentary *Matthew: A Commentary* (Minneapolis: Fortress, 2001, 2005, 2007) is distinctive in two ways. It offers thought-provoking questions for theological discernment and pastoral reflection in the "History of Interpretation" section after each passage, and it attempts to connect the claims of the Scripture to the practice of our life through honest wrestling with the difficult texts of the Bible, the competing interpretations of the church, and the harsh reality of life today.

ABOUT THE AUTHOR

John Y. H. Yieh is professor of New Testament at Virginia Theological Seminary and an ordained minister in the Presbyterian Church (USA). He has served as president of the Mid-Atlantic Regional Society of Biblical Literature, and is president of the Ethnic Chinese Biblical Colloquium. He is the author of *A Concise Greek-Chinese Dictionary of the New Testament* (Singapore: United Bible Societies, 1989), *One Teacher: Jesus' Teaching Role in Matthew's Gospel* (Berlin: de Gruyter, 2004), *Making Sense of the Sermon on the Mount* (Cambridge: Grove, 2007), and the coauthor of *Revelation,* Immersion Biblical Studies (Nashville: Abingdon, 2011). He has also published several articles in *The New Interpreter's Dictionary of the Bible* and *The Encyclopedia of the Bible and Its Reception*, and several essays on New Testament studies and Chinese biblical interpretation. He is a frequent speaker at churches in the Washington, DC, area and has lectured at universities and seminaries in the United States, Britain, Tanzania, Singapore, Taiwan, Hong Kong, and China.